# GoodFood
## Healthy family food

10 9 8 7 6 5 4 3 2 1

Published in 2013 by BBC Books, an imprint of Ebury Publishing
A Random House Group company

Photographs © BBC Worldwide 2013
Recipes © BBC Worldwide 2013
Book design © Woodlands Books Ltd 2013
All recipes contained in this book first appeared in BBC *Good Food* magazine.

The Random House Group Limited
Reg. No. 954009

Addresses for companies within the Random House Group can be found at www.randomhouse.co.uk

A CIP catalogue record for this book is available from the British Library

The Random House Group Limited supports The Forest Stewardship Council® (FSC®), the leading international forest certification organisation. Our books carrying the FSC label are printed on FSC® certified paper. FSC is the only forest certification scheme endorsed by the leading environmental organisations, including Greenpeace. Our paper procurement policy can be found at www.randomhouse.co.uk/environment

To buy books by your favourite authors and register for offers visit www.randomhouse.co.uk

Printed and bound by Firmengruppe APPL, aprinta druck, Wemding, Germany
Colour origination by Dot Gradations Ltd, UK

Commissioning Editor: Muna Reyal
Project Editors: Joe Cottington and Sarah Watling
Designer: Kathryn Gammon
Production: Rebecca Jones
Picture Researcher: Gabby Harrington

ISBN: 9781849906241

## Picture credits

BBC *Good Food* magazine and BBC Books would like to thank the following people for providing photos. While every effort has been made to trace and acknowledge all photographers, we should like to apologise should there be any errors or omissions.

Marie-Louise Avery p201; Peter Cassidy p195, p197, p207; Jean Cazals p11; Will Heap p15, p139, p141, p143, p177; Lara Holmes p121; Gareth Morgans p37, p47, p79, p97, p105, p205; David Munns p27, p33, p35, p55, p57, p63, p69, p67, p71, p73, p83, p85, p91, p93, p101, p103, p107, p113, p125, p127, p145, p149, p155, p157, p167, p171, p173, p183, p185, p187, p203, p211; Myles New p19, p29, p31, p41, p45, p49, p51, p59, p75, p89, p193, p199; Stuart Ovenden p17, p39, p77, p95, p109, p111, p147; Lis Parsons p21, p43, p81, p87, p99, p115, p123, p129, p131, p133, p153, p159, p161, p179, p181; Charlie Richards p61, p169; Howard Shooter p65, p135, p175; Maja Smend p25; Roger Stowell p23; Yuki Sugiura p117, p165; Philip Webb p189; Jon Whitaker p13, p53, p119, p137, p151, p163, p209

All the recipes in this book were created by the editorial team at *Good Food* and by regular contributors to BBC Magazines.

*everyday*

# GoodFood
## Healthy family food

Editor **Cassie Best**

# Contents

Introduction 6

Breakfasts
10

Nibbles & snacks
46

Light lunches
76

Everyday dinners
114

Better than a
takeaway
152

Sweet treats
188

Index  212

# Introduction

Feeding your family a healthy, well-balanced diet can be hard work when you are trying to juggle a busy household schedule. But taking the time to ensure you put the right food on the table and in your children's tummies will make you a happier, healthier family.

The secret to eating well is not only planning ahead to make sure you have a fridge stocked with fresh fruit, veg and lean meat but also ensuring that you have plenty of healthy recipes up your sleeve. That's why we've put together this handy book of quick and easy ideas to turn the contents of your veg drawer into meals the whole family will enjoy.

Children can be picky when it comes to eating their veg, and all too often they opt for foods that are high in sugar and saturated fat. By introducing a little colour, new tastes and textures to their plates they will begin to enjoy trying new foods. Most of the recipes in this book are suitable for children to help out with. Get smaller children to snip herbs with small scissors or mix salad dressings – any involvement in cooking will make them much more likely to give it a try.

Processed ready meals and takeaways are often the quick option when you are pressed for time, but generally they don't contain much that's good for you! We know that takeaways are most people's downfall when it comes to eating well, so we've included a chapter called *Better than a takeaway*, so you and your family can enjoy your Friday-night favourites without the guilt.

The recipes in this book all fall under the healthy category by containing less than 5g saturated fat, 15g sugar and 1.5g salt. They have all been triple-tested by the *Good Food* team and are all easy to follow, giving you healthy and delicious meals every time.

*Cassie*

Cassie Best
*Good Food* magazine

# Notes and conversion tables

NOTES ON THE RECIPES
- Eggs are large in the UK and Australia and extra large in America unless stated otherwise.
- Wash fresh produce before preparation.
- Recipes contain nutritional analyses for 'sugar', which means the total sugar content including all natural sugars in the ingredients, unless stated otherwise.

## OVEN TEMPERATURES

| Gas | °C | °C Fan | °F | Oven temp. |
|-----|-----|--------|-----|----------------|
| ¼ | 110 | 90 | 225 | Very cool |
| ½ | 120 | 100 | 250 | Very cool |
| 1 | 140 | 120 | 275 | Cool or slow |
| 2 | 150 | 130 | 300 | Cool or slow |
| 3 | 160 | 140 | 325 | Warm |
| 4 | 180 | 160 | 350 | Moderate |
| 5 | 190 | 170 | 375 | Moderately hot |
| 6 | 200 | 180 | 400 | Fairly hot |
| 7 | 220 | 200 | 425 | Hot |
| 8 | 230 | 210 | 450 | Very hot |
| 9 | 240 | 220 | 475 | Very hot |

APPROXIMATE WEIGHT CONVERSIONS
- All the recipes in this book list both imperial and metric measurements. Conversions are approximate and have been rounded up or down. Follow one set of measurements only; do not mix the two.
- Cup measurements, which are used by cooks in Australia and America, have not been listed here as they vary from ingredient to ingredient. Kitchen scales should be used to measure dry/solid ingredients.

*Good Food* is concerned about sustainable sourcing and animal welfare. Where possible humanely reared meats, sustainably caught fish (see fishonline. org for further information from the Marine Conservation Society) and free-range chickens and eggs are used when recipes are originally tested.

SPOON MEASURES

Spoon measurements are level unless otherwise specified.

- 1 teaspoon (tsp) = 5ml
- 1 tablespoon (tbsp) = 15ml
- 1 Australian tablespoon = 20ml (cooks in Australia should measure 3 teaspoons where 1 tablespoon is specified in a recipe)

APPROXIMATE LIQUID CONVERSIONS

| metric | imperial | AUS | US |
| --- | --- | --- | --- |
| 50ml | 2fl oz | ¼ cup | ¼ cup |
| 125ml | 4fl oz | ½ cup | ½ cup |
| 175ml | 6fl oz | ¾ cup | ¾ cup |
| 225ml | 8fl oz | 1 cup | 1 cup |
| 300ml | 10fl oz/½ pint | ½ pint | 1¼ cups |
| 450ml | 16fl oz | 2 cups | 2 cups/1 pint |
| 600ml | 20fl oz/1 pint | 1 pint | 2½ cups |
| 1 litre | 35fl oz/1¾ pints | 1¾ pints | 1 quart |

# Good-for-you granola

*Most granolas are packed with refined sugars, which leave your blood-sugar levels rocketing. This healthier version contains less sugar than shop-bought varieties.*

**TAKES 35 MINUTES • SERVES 15**

2 tbsp vegetable oil
125ml/4fl oz maple syrup
2 tbsp clear honey
1 tsp vanilla extract
300g/10oz rolled oats
50g/2oz sunflower seeds
4 tbsp sesame seeds
50g/2oz pumpkin seeds
100g/4oz flaked almonds
100g/4oz dried berries (find them in the baking aisle)
50g/2oz coconut flakes or desiccated coconut
cold milk or natural yogurt, to serve

**1** Heat oven to 150C/130C fan/gas 2. Mix the oil, maple syrup, honey and vanilla in a large bowl. Tip in all the remaining ingredients, except the dried berries and coconut, and mix well.

**2** Tip the granola on to two baking sheets and spread evenly. Bake for 15 minutes, then mix in the dried fruit and coconut, and bake for 10–15 minutes more. Remove and scrape on to a flat tray to cool. Serve with cold milk or yogurt. The granola can be stored in an airtight container for up to a month.

PER SERVING 259 kcals, protein 6g, carbs 28g, fat 15g, sat fat 3g, fibre 3g, sugar 13g, salt 0.02g

# Apple & linseed porridge

*Ground linseed is full of stomach-friendly fibre and is a great source of omega-3, making this porridge the perfect way to start the day.*

**TAKES 12 MINUTES • SERVES 4**

100g/4oz porridge oats

2 eating apples, peeled and grated

½ tsp ground cinnamon, plus extra for sprinkling

500ml/18fl oz skimmed milk

2 tbsp ground linseed

150g pot probiotic yogurt

drizzle honey or agave syrup

**1** In a medium pan, mix the oats, apples, cinnamon and milk. Bring to the boil, stirring occasionally, then turn down the heat and cook for 4–5 minutes, stirring constantly.

**2** Stir in the ground linseed, then divide among four breakfast bowls. Top each with a dollop of yogurt, a drizzle of honey or agave syrup and a sprinkle more cinnamon.

PER SERVING 236 kcals, protein 12g, carbs 29g, fat 6g, sat fat 2g, fibre 6g, sugar 15g, salt 0.2g

# Grapefruit, agave & pistachio salad

*Start the day with this nutrient-packed, low-fat breakfast. You can substitute the nuts for your favourite variety, if you prefer.*

**TAKES 5 MINUTES • SERVES 2**

1 pink grapefruit
1 white grapefruit
1 tbsp agave nectar
1 tsp chopped pistachio nuts

**1** Segment the grapefruits, removing as much of the pith as possible. Divide the segments between two bowls and top each with a drizzle of agave nectar and scatter over the pistachios.

PER SERVING 107 kcals, protein 2g, carbs 21g, fat 1g, sat fat none, fibre 2g, sugar 12g, salt none

# Summer fruit compote

*Keep a batch of this fruity compote in the fridge for a quick breakfast – it's perfect swirled into some natural yogurt.*

**TAKES 15 MINUTES • SERVES 6**

4 large plums, stoned and cut into wedges
200g/7oz punnet blueberries
zest and juice 1 orange
1 tbsp light soft brown sugar
clear honey, to drizzle
150g punnet raspberries
natural yogurt, to serve (optional)

**1** Cook the plums and blueberries in a small pan with the orange zest and juice, sugar and 4 tablespoons water until slightly softened but not mushy. Gently stir in the raspberries and cook for 1 minute more.
**2** Remove from the heat and allow to cool to room temperature. Serve with yogurt and a drizzle of honey, if you like.

---

PER SERVING 64 kcals, protein 1g, carbs 14g, fat 0.3g, sat fat none, fibre 3g, sugar 14g, salt none

# One-pan summer eggs

*A great dish to satisfy your hunger at breakfast, lunch or dinner.*

**TAKES 20 MINUTES** • **SERVES 2**

1 tbsp olive oil

400g/14oz courgettes (about 2 large ones), chopped into small chunks

200g/7oz pack cherry tomatoes, halved

1 garlic clove, crushed

2 medium eggs

few basil leaves, to garnish

crusty bread, to serve

**1** Heat the oil in a non-stick frying pan, then add the courgettes. Fry for 5 minutes, stirring every so often until they start to soften, add the tomatoes and garlic, then cook for a few minutes more. Stir in a little seasoning, then make two gaps in the mix and crack in the eggs.

**2** Cover the pan with a lid or a sheet of foil, then cook for 2–3 minutes until the eggs are done to your liking. Scatter over a few basil leaves and serve with crusty bread.

PER SERVING 196 kcals, protein 12g, carbs 7g, fat 13g, sat fat 3g, fibre 3g, sugar 6g, salt 0.25g

# Spiced scrambled eggs

*Using a mixture of whole eggs and egg whites dramatically cuts the amount of fat in this recipe.*

**TAKES 30 MINUTES ● SERVES 2**

knob butter
1 small onion, chopped
1 red chilli, deseeded and chopped
2 whole eggs, 2 egg whites, beaten
splash skimmed milk
handful cherry tomatoes, chopped
small handful coriander, leaves picked
buttered toast, to serve

**1** Melt the butter in a frying pan set over a medium heat and soften the onion and chilli. Stir in the beaten eggs and a splash of milk, and stir with a wooden spoon. When nearly scrambled, gently stir in a good handful of diced tomatoes followed by most of the coriander leaves. Season, scatter with the remaining coriander leaves and eat on buttered toast.

PER SERVING 153 kcals, protein 11g, carbs 3g, fat 11g, sat fat 4g, fibre 1g, sugar 3g, salt 0.4g

# Asparagus soldiers with soft-boiled eggs

*Give the classic breakfast dish a twist by serving the eggs with young asparagus tips instead of toast soldiers, when in season.*

**TAKES 20 MINUTES** ● **SERVES 4**

1 tbsp olive oil
50g/2oz fine dry breadcrumbs
pinch each chilli powder and paprika
16–20 asparagus spears
4 medium eggs

**1** Heat the oil in a pan, add the breadcrumbs, then fry until crisp and golden. Season with the spices and some flaky sea salt, then leave to cool.
**2** Cook the asparagus in a large pan of boiling salted water for 3–5 minutes until tender. At the same time, boil the eggs for 4 minutes.
**3** Put each egg in an egg cup on a plate. Drain the asparagus and divide among plates. Scatter the crumbs over the asparagus and serve.

---

PER SERVING 186 kcals, protein 12g, carbs 12g, fat 10g, sat fat 2g, fibre 2g, sugar 3g, salt 0.72g

# Dippy egg with Marmite soldiers

*Start the day the right way with this quick, easy and nutritious breakfast.*

**TAKES 10 MINUTES** ● **SERVES 2**

2 medium eggs
4 slices wholemeal bread
2 tsp Marmite
1 tbsp mixed seeds

**1** Bring a pan of water to a simmer then add the eggs and cook for 3–4 minutes.
**2** Meanwhile, toast the bread and spread with Marmite. To serve, cut into soldiers and dip them into the egg, then into a few mixed seeds to coat.

PER SERVING 372 kcals, protein 17g, carbs 31g, fat 21g, sat fat 5g, fibre 4g, sugar 2g, salt 1.09g

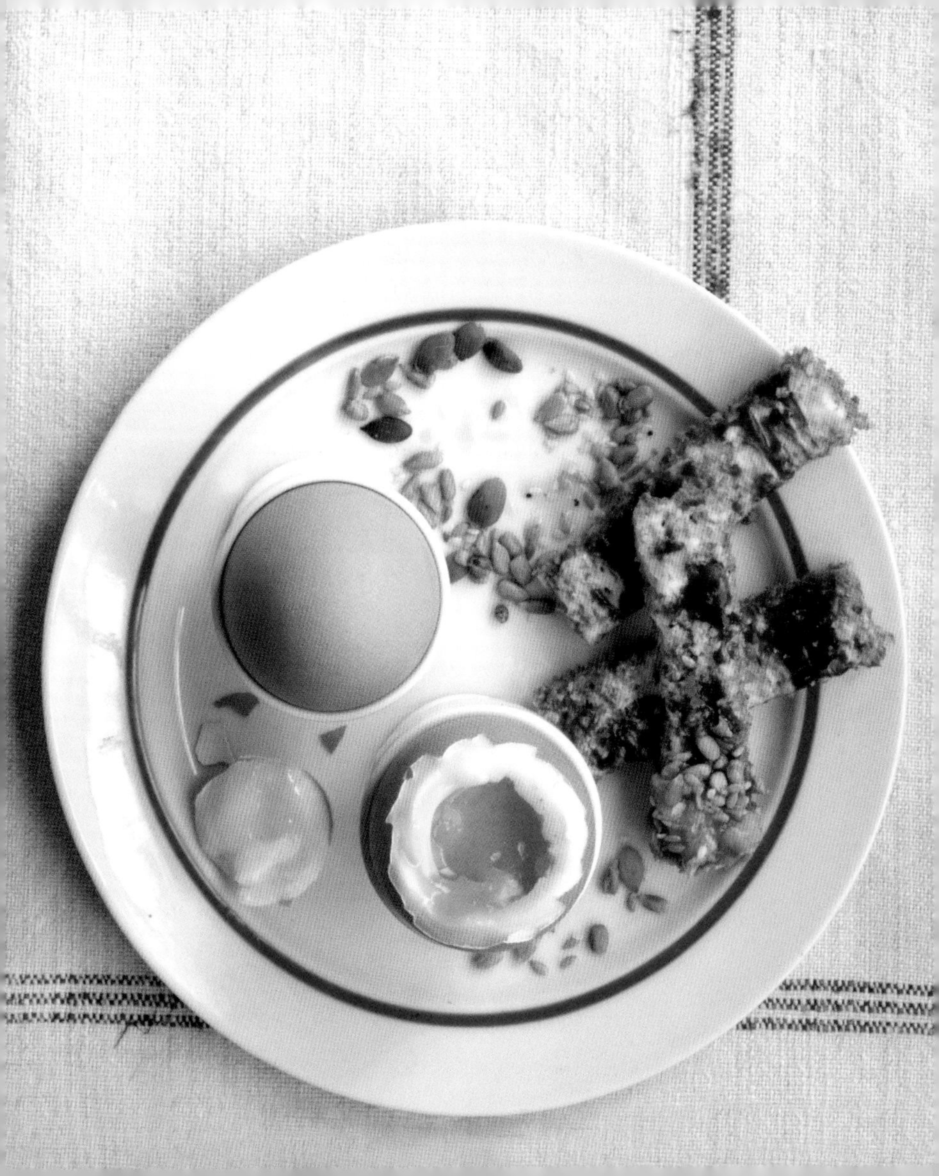

# Vegan tomato & mushroom pancakes

*If you're not a vegan, simply replace the soya ingredients with non-vegan alternatives.*

**TAKES 35 MINUTES** ● **SERVES 2**

140g/5oz self-raising flour
1 tsp soya flour
400ml/14fl oz soya milk
vegetable oil, for frying

**FOR THE TOPPING**

2 tbsp vegetable oil
250g/9oz button mushrooms
250g/9oz cherry tomatoes, halved
2 tbsp soya cream or soya milk
handful pine nuts
snipped chives, to garnish

**1** Sift the flours and a pinch of salt into a blender. Add the soya milk and blend to make a smooth batter.

**2** Heat a little oil in a medium non-stick frying pan until very hot. Pour about 3 tablespoons of the batter into the pan and cook over a medium heat until bubbles appear on the surface of the pancake. Flip the pancake over with a palette knife and cook the other side until golden brown. Repeat with the remaining batter, keeping the cooked pancakes warm as you go. You will make about eight.

**3** For the topping, heat the oil in a frying pan. Cook the mushrooms until tender, add the tomatoes and cook for a couple of minutes. Pour in the soya cream or milk and pine nuts, then gently cook until combined. Divide the pancakes between two plates, spoon over the tomatoes and mushrooms and scatter with chives.

PER SERVING 609 kcals, protein 18g, carbs 59g, fat 35g, sat fat 4g, fibre 6g, sugar 6g, salt 0.87g

# Plate-sized pancakes

*These pancakes are low in fat, so you really can have your cake and eat it too! Serve with fresh fruit or a little lean crispy bacon and a dribble of maple syrup.*

**TAKES 30 MINUTES ● MAKES 6**

300g/10oz self-raising flour
1 tsp baking powder
1 tbsp caster sugar
2 medium eggs
300ml/½ pint skimmed milk
splash of oil

**TO SERVE**

blueberries, or pancetta or lean
    smoked bacon and maple syrup
    (optional)

**1** Mix the flour, baking powder and sugar in a large bowl with a small pinch of salt. Crack in the eggs and whisk until smooth. Add the milk while whisking.

**2** Heat a splash of oil in a non-stick frying pan until hot. Add ladlefuls of batter to make six large pancakes. Cook until bubbles start to form on the surface, then flip over and cook the other side. Eat straight away or keep them warm in a low oven. Serve the pancakes with blueberries or crispy pancetta or smoked bacon, drizzled with a little maple syrup, if you like.

---

PER PANCAKE 251 kcals, protein 8g, carbs 43g, fat 5g, sat fat 2g, fibre 2g, sugar 8g, salt 1g

# Fruitburst muffins

*You can make a batch of these muffins and pop them in the freezer. Simply take out as many as you need the night before and leave them to defrost.*

**TAKES 50 MINUTES ● MAKES 12**

225g/8oz plain flour
2 tsp baking powder
2 eggs
50g/2oz butter, melted, plus extra for greasing
175ml/6fl oz skimmed milk
100ml/3½fl oz clear honey
140g/5oz fresh blueberries
85g/3oz dried cranberries
140g/5oz seedless raisins
140g/5oz dried apricots, chopped
1 tsp orange zest
1 tsp ground cinnamon

**1** Heat oven to 200C/180C fan/gas 6 and very lightly butter a 12-hole muffin tin. Sift the flour and baking powder into a bowl. In another bowl, lightly beat the eggs, then stir in the melted butter, milk and honey. Add to the flour with the remaining ingredients. Combine quickly without overworking (it's fine if there are some lumps left – you want it gloopy rather than fluid). Spoon the mixture into the muffin tin. Bake for 20–25 minutes until well risen and pale golden on top.
**2** Leave them in the tin for a few minutes before turning out. When cool, they'll keep in an airtight tin for 2 days. They can also be frozen for up to 1 month.

PER MUFFIN 243 kcals, protein 5g, carbs 41g, fat 8g, sat fat 3g, fibre 2g, sugar 6g, salt 0.59g

# Spiced fruit loaf

*This fruity loaf is great spread with a little jam and served with a mug of tea.*

**TAKES 50 MINUTES, PLUS SOAKING, RISING AND PROVING • MAKES 2 × 900G/2LB LOAVES, EACH CUTS INTO 8 SLICES**

200g/7oz dried fruit (we used apricots, figs, dates and sultanas, chopped – except the sultanas)
50g/2oz glacé cherries, chopped
juice 1 orange
450g/1lb strong white flour, plus extra for dusting
2 × 7g sachets easy-blend yeast
50g/2oz caster sugar
1 tsp salt
1½ tsp ground cinnamon
1 tsp ground ginger
150ml/¼ pint warm milk
1 egg, beaten
50g/2oz butter, melted, plus extra for greasing
oil, for greasing

**1** Soak the dried fruit and cherries in the orange juice for 30 minutes, then strain, reserving the juice.

**2** Put the flour, yeast, caster sugar and salt in to a mixing bowl with the spices and soaked fruit, and mix. Make a well in the centre. Pour in the warm milk, reserved orange juice, beaten egg and melted butter. Mix to form a dough – use a wooden spoon and finish with your hands. If the dough is dry, add warm water; if it's wet, add more flour.

**3** Knead on a floured surface until springy. Transfer to a greased bowl and cover with a damp tea towel. Leave in a warm place to rise for about 1 hour.

**4** Knock the dough back by kneading briefly. Dust two 900g loaf tins with flour. Halve the dough, shape each half into an oval, then pop them in to the tins. Cover both with a damp tea towel and leave in a warm place for about 20 minutes. Heat oven to 180C/160C fan/gas 4.

**5** Bake for 20 minutes, then cool in the tins before turning out and slicing.

PER SLICE 190 kcals, protein 5g, carbs 36g, fat 4g, sat fat 2g, fibre 2g, sugar 14g, salt 0.35g

# Apricot, honey & pistachio bars

*These bars are perfect for an on-the-go breakfast or a mid-morning snack.*

**TAKES 50 MINUTES**
- **SLICES INTO 16 BARS**

140g/5oz butter
140g/5oz soft brown sugar
2 tbsp clear honey
175g/6oz rolled oats
75g/2½oz shelled pistachio nuts,
    chopped
140g/5oz dried apricots, chopped

**1** Put the butter, sugar and honey in a small pan, then heat gently until melted.
**2** Tip the oats, pistachios and apricots into a medium bowl. Pour over the melted-butter mixture and stir to combine.
**3** Transfer to a 20cm-square greased and lined baking tin and cook at 160C/140C fan/gas 4 for 35–40 minutes. Remove and cool in the tin, then slice into 16. Will keep in an airtight container for up to 3 days.

PER BAR 193 kcals, protein 3g, carbs 22g, fat 11g, sat fat 5g, fibre 2g, sugar 15g, salt 0.13g

# Peanut butter & banana toastie

*A sweet treat for hungry kids, perfect to fill their tummies before a long day at school.*

**TAKES 10 MINUTES ● SERVES 1**

2 slices granary or brown bread
½ banana
½ tsp ground cinnamon
1 tbsp crunchy peanut butter

**1** Toast the bread and slice the banana. Layer the banana on one slice of toast and dust with cinnamon. Spread the second slice of bread with peanut butter, then sandwich the two together and eat straight away.

PER SERVING 271 kcals, protein 10g, carbs 36g, fat 9g, sat fat 2g, fibre 4g, sugar 10g, salt 1g

# Veggie breakfast bake

*A big cooked breakfast is a great way to start the day. This one is low in fat but high in flavour and will keep you going until lunchtime.*

**TAKES 45 MINUTES • SERVES 4**

4 large field mushrooms
8 tomatoes, halved
1 garlic clove, thinly sliced
2 tsp olive oil
200g bag spinach leaves
4 eggs

**1** Heat oven to 200C/180C fan/gas 6. Put the mushrooms and tomatoes into four ovenproof dishes or on to a baking sheet. Divide the garlic among the mushrooms and tomatoes, drizzle over the oil and some seasoning, then bake for 10 minutes.

**2** Meanwhile, put the spinach into a large colander then pour over a kettle of boiling water to wilt it. Squeeze out any excess water, then add the spinach to the dishes or tray. Make little gaps between the vegetables and crack an egg into each space. Return to the oven and cook for a further 8–10 minutes or until the eggs are cooked to your liking.

PER SERVING 127 kcals, protein 9g, carbs 5g, fat 8g, sat fat 2g, fibre 3g, sugar 5g, salt 0.4g

# Smoky bean, bacon & eggy bread bake

*This is a great one-pot breakfast dish to serve up at the weekend. The beans can be made ahead and chilled until you're ready to bake.*

**TAKES 1 HOUR 10 MINUTES**
● **SERVES 8**

3 × 400g cans haricot beans, drained and rinsed
500g/1lb 2oz passata
½ tbsp sweet smoked paprika
1 tbsp red wine vinegar
1 tbsp dark muscovado sugar
100g/4oz bacon lardons
5 medium eggs
125ml/4fl oz skimmed milk
8 slices white or brown bread, crusts removed and halved to make triangles

**1** Heat oven to 220C/200C fan/gas 7. Tip the beans into a large baking dish with the passata, paprika, vinegar and sugar. Season and mix well. Scatter the lardons over the top, cover with foil and bake for 30 minutes.

**2** Remove the beans from the oven, take off the foil and stir well. Return to the oven, uncovered, for 10 minutes to crisp up the bacon. You can now cool and chill the beans for up to 2 days, or freeze for up to 3 months. Just defrost and warm through before continuing.

**3** Whisk the eggs and milk with some seasoning. Dip the bread triangles into most of the egg mix, then layer them over the surface of the beans. Pour the rest of the egg over the bread and cook for 20 minutes, or until the bread is puffed and golden.

---

PER SERVING 245 kcals, protein 15g, carbs 31g, fat 6.5g, sat fat 2g, fibre 9g, sugar 7.5g, salt 0.8g

# Better-than-baked-beans with potato wedges

*Kids will love these homemade beans – they are so much better than the tinned variety. Serve with toast or potato wedges.*

**TAKES 45 MINUTES ● SERVES 2**

1 tsp oil
1 onion, halved and thinly sliced
2 rashers lean bacon, cut into largish
    pieces
1 tsp light soft brown sugar
400g can chopped tomatoes
200ml/7fl oz stock, from a cube
400g can cannellini, butter or haricot
    beans in water, drained and rinsed

**FOR THE WEDGES**

1 tbsp plain flour
½ tsp cayenne pepper, paprika or mild
    chilli powder
1 tsp dried mixed herbs
2 baking potatoes, each cut into
    8 wedges
2 tsp oil

**1** Heat oven to 200C/180C fan/gas 6. For the wedges, mix the flour, cayenne, paprika or chilli powder and the herbs, add some salt and pepper, then toss with the potatoes and oil until well coated. Tip into a roasting tin, then bake for about 35 minutes until crisp and cooked through.

**2** Meanwhile, heat the oil in a non-stick pan, then gently fry the onion and bacon together for 5–10 minutes until the onions are softened and just starting to turn golden. Stir in the sugar, tomatoes, stock and seasoning to taste, then simmer the sauce for 5 minutes. Add the beans, then simmer for another 5 minutes until the sauce has thickened. Serve with the wedges.

PER SERVING 399 kcals, protein 19g, carbs 60g, fat 11g, sat fat 2g, fibre none, sugar 15g, salt 1.14g

# Classic kedgeree

*This Anglo-Indian favourite is full of flavour – the perfect breakfast after a heavy night out!*

**TAKES 45 MINUTES • SERVES 6**

3 tbsp vegetable oil

1 large onion, finely chopped

1 tsp ground coriander

1 tsp turmeric powder

2 tsp curry powder

200g/7oz long grain rice, rinsed under cold water

6 medium eggs

400ml/14fl oz milk

300g/10oz undyed smoked haddock

2 bay leaves

small handful coriander and parsley, chopped

**1** Heat the oil and cook the onion in a pan with a well-fitting lid until soft but not coloured. Add the spices and some salt, and continue to cook until golden and fragrant, about 4 minutes. Sprinkle over the rice and stir well so that all the grains are coated. Stir in 400ml/14fl oz water, increase the heat, cover, then bring to the boil. Once boiling, lower to a simmer for 10 minutes. Turn off the heat and leave to steam, covered, for 20 minutes.

**2** Put the eggs in a pan and cover with cold water, then put over a high heat and bring to the boil. Simmer for 3 minutes for soft or 5–6 minutes for hard-boiled. Plunge into cold water until cool enough to peel, then quarter them.

**3** Meanwhile, pour the milk over the haddock and the bay leaves in a pan and simmer for 5–8 minutes. Remove from the milk, discard the skin and flake the fish. Stir the fish, herbs and some seasoning into the rice. Top with the eggs.

PER SERVING 324 kcals, protein 20g, carbs 33g, fat 13g, sat fat 3g, fibre 1g, sugar 2g, salt 1.21g

# Almond butter

*This healthy butter is great spread on to low-fat malt bread as a quick snack or speedy breakfast.*

**TAKES 25 MINUTES**
● **MAKES 300G/10OZ JAR**
300g/10oz skin-on almonds
good drizzle clear honey
malt loaf or wholegrain bread, to serve

**1** Heat oven to 190C/170C fan/gas 5. Spread the almonds on a baking sheet and roast for 10 minutes. Remove and allow to cool.
**2** Put the cooled almonds into a food processor and whizz for 12 minutes, stopping every so often to scrape the sides down, and finish with a drizzle of honey. Serve spread over malt loaf or wholegrain bread. Will keep in the fridge for up to 3 weeks.

PER TBSP 93 kcals, protein 3g, carbs 1g, fat 8g, sat fat 1g, fibre 1g, sugar 1g, salt none

# Warm Mexican bean dip

*A superhealthy, easy and freezable dip that counts towards your 5-a-day. What more could you want?*

**TAKES 30 MINUTES** • **SERVES 8**

1 onion, chopped

1 tbsp olive oil

1 tsp soft brown sugar

1 tsp wine vinegar

1 tsp Cajun seasoning

400g can mixed beans, drained and
  rinsed

400g can chopped tomatoes with garlic

chopped avocado, to garnish (optional)

tortilla chips, for dipping (optional)

**1** Fry the chopped onion in olive oil until soft. Add the soft brown sugar, wine vinegar and Cajun seasoning. Cook for 1 minute then add the mixed beans and chopped tomatoes with garlic. Simmer for 10–15 minutes until the sauce has thickened, then season.

**2** Serve the dip in a bowl, scattered with chopped avocado and with tortilla chips alongside for dipping, if you like.

PER SERVING 144 kcals, protein 6g, carbs 16g, fat 7g, sat fat 2g, fibre 3g, sugar 3g, salt 0.76g

# Courgette & minty bean dip

*Pack up this fresh and minty dip with crudités and breadsticks for a summery picnic.*

**TAKES 35 MINUTES** ● **SERVES 4**

2 tbsp olive oil

1 courgette, finely diced

2 garlic cloves, chopped

400g can cannellini beans, drained and rinsed

juice ½ lemon

170g pot 0% fat Greek yogurt

2 tbsp chopped mint leaves

**1** Heat the oil in a pan. Fry the courgette and garlic with a little seasoning until the courgette is tender.

**2** Set aside a couple of tablespoons of the courgette and tip the rest into a bowl with the beans, lemon juice, yogurt and mint. Whizz until smooth with a hand blender, then spoon into a bowl or food container and top with the reserved courgette to finish.

PER SERVING 352 kcals, protein 12g, carbs 45g, fat 13g, sat fat 3g, fibre 3g, sugar 7g, salt 1.5g

# Pea, mint & chilli dip

*This quick and nutritious dip will keep well in the fridge for 2 days.*

**TAKES 5 MINUTES** • **SERVES 6**

400g/14oz frozen peas, defrosted
100g/4oz fat-free natural yogurt
juice 1 lemon
1 tsp ground cumin
small handful mint leaves
1 small red chilli, deseeded and
   chopped
4 wholemeal pitta breads
500g/1lb 2oz carrots, cut into batons

**1** Whizz the peas, yogurt, lemon juice, cumin, mint and chilli together in a food processor to a texture you like. Divide among plastic tubs to pack into lunchboxes or tip into a serving bowl.
**2** Lightly toast the pittas, then cut into wedges and serve with the dip and carrot batons.

PER SERVING 187 kcals, protein 10g, carbs 32g, fat 2g, sat fat 0.4g, fibre 8g, sugar 10g, salt 0.5g

# Chinese-spiced seed mix

*Keep a jar of this seed mix in the cupboard or pack into tubs to snack on throughout the day at work.*

**TAKES 20 MINUTES • SERVES 2**

1 egg white
2 tsp Chinese five spice powder
75g/2½oz each sunflower and pumpkin
   seeds

**1** Heat oven to 150C/130C fan/gas 2. Lightly whisk the egg white, then add the Chinese five spice and ½ teaspoon salt. Add the sunflower and pumpkin seeds, and coat well. Spread out in a single layer on a lightly oiled baking sheet and bake for 12 minutes. Cool before eating.

PER SERVING 437 kcals, protein 18g, carbs 12g, fat 35g, sat fat 5g, fibre 6g, sugar 1g, salt 1.4g

# Raspberry-oat traybake

*You can replace the raspberries in this fruity traybake with your favourite fruit – just be sure to cook any harder fruits to soften them first.*

**TAKES 30 MINUTES • CUTS INTO 16 SLICES**

150g punnet fresh raspberries
50g/2oz butter, plus extra for greasing
75g/2½oz clear honey
200g/7oz rolled oats
50g/2oz ground almonds
½ tsp almond extract

**1** Heat oven to 220C/200C fan/gas 7. Grease a 20cm-square baking tin. Mash the raspberries roughly in a bowl and set aside.

**2** In a medium pan, melt the butter and honey with a pinch of salt. Take off the heat, then stir in the oats, ground almonds and almond extract. Mix until they are coated in the butter-and-honey mixture.

**3** Press half the oat mix in an even layer in the baking tin. Spread the mashed raspberries on top, then spoon the remaining oat mix on top and smooth with the back of a spoon. Bake for 10–12 minutes or until golden. Remove from the oven and leave to cool before slicing into 16.

PER SERVING 111 kcals, protein 2g, carbs 13g, fat 6g, sat fat 2g, fibre 1g, sugar 4g, salt 0.06g

# Scandi cheese & crackers

*Perfect for lunchboxes, cool cream cheese spread on to wheaty biscuits is a real Scandi classic.*

**TAKES 10 MINUTES • SERVES 1**
2 tbsp low-fat soft cheese
few snipped chives
few cornichons
wholewheat biscuits or crackers

**1** Dollop low-fat soft cheese, snipped chives and a few cornichons into a tub. Eat with wholewheat biscuits or crackers.

PER SERVING 246 kcals, protein 11g, carbs 32g, fat 8g, sat fat 3g, fibre 3g, sugar 2g, salt 1.3g

# Spicy chickpeas

*Get the whole family snacking on this low-fat alternative to peanuts.*

**TAKES 35 MINUTES • SERVES 4**

400g can chickpeas, drained, rinsed
   and dried
1 tsp vegetable oil
1 tbsp chilli powder

**1** Heat oven to 220C/200C fan/gas 7. Tip the chickpeas into a bowl with the vegetable oil and chilli powder, and mix until the chickpeas are coated with chilli.
**2** Transfer to a baking sheet and spread out the chickpeas, then cook for 25 minutes. Remove from the oven and allow to cool before serving.

PER SERVING 80 kcals, protein 4.5g, carbs 10g, fat 2g, sat fat none, fibre 3g, salt 0.41g

# Turkey & avocado toasts

*Toast toppers can make a great protein-packed snack; for a variation you could swap the turkey for ham or chicken, if you like.*

**TAKES 15 MINUTES • SERVES 2**

1 avocado
juice ½ lime
2–3 small slices ciabatta bread
100g/4oz turkey slices

**1** Halve and stone the avocado then scrape out the flesh into a bowl. Squeeze in the lime, season, then mash roughly with a fork.
**2** Toast the ciabatta, spread with mashed avocado, top with turkey and finish with freshly ground black pepper.

PER SERVING 208 kcals, protein 15g, carbs 12g, fat 11g, sat fat 2g, fibre 2g, sugar 1g, salt 1.3g

# Oaty energy cookies

*A great snack to serve with a glass of milk if you need a quick boost.*

**TAKES 40 MINUTES ● MAKES 6**

50g/2oz butter, softened
50g/2oz light soft brown sugar
2 tbsp condensed milk (look for it in
    tubes)
50g/2oz rolled oats
50g/2oz dried apricots, chopped
85g/3oz self-raising flour

**1** Heat oven to 150C/130C fan/gas 2. Line a baking sheet with baking parchment. Put the butter and sugar in a mixing bowl, and beat well with a wooden spoon. Add the condensed milk, beat well, then add the oats and apricots, and mix well again. Finally, add the flour and mix until it starts to resemble a dough.

**2** Bring the dough together into one big ball, then break into six equal-sized lumps. Roll each into a ball, then squash on to the baking parchment with the palm of your hand.

**3** Bake for 25–30 minutes until golden at the edges. Leave to cool on the tin. The cookies will keep in an airtight container for up to 3 days.

PER COOKIE 201 kcals, protein 4g, carbs 28g, fat 8g, sat fat 5g, fibre 2g, sugar 14g, salt 0.3g

# Flowerpot bread

*Breadmaking is a great skill to teach kids to get them interested in cooking. Bake these little loaves in flowerpots for extra appeal and top with your favourite topping.*

**TAKES 50 MINUTES • MAKES 5**

500g/1lb 2oz granary, wholemeal or
  strong white bread flour
1 × 7g sachet fast-action dried yeast
2 tbsp olive oil, plus extra for greasing
  the flowerpots
1 tbsp clear honey
a little milk or oil, for brushing

**PLUS ANY OF THESE TOPPINGS**

1 tbsp pumpkin, sunflower, sesame or
  poppy seeds
1 tbsp chopped leaves rosemary,
  thyme, oregano, chives or basil
1 tbsp chopped pitted olives or
  sundried tomatoes
½ tsp chilli flakes

**YOU WILL ALSO NEED**

5 small clean clay flowerpots, baking
  parchment and cling film

**1** Tip the flour, yeast and 1 teaspoon salt into a large bowl. Pour in 300ml/½ pint warm water, the olive oil and honey. Mix with a wooden spoon until the mixture clumps together, then tip out on to a work surface. Use your hands to stretch and knead the dough for about 10 minutes or until it's smooth and springy. Add a little extra flour if the dough feels too sticky.

**2** Brush the flowerpots with oil and line the sides and base with baking parchment. Divide the dough into five pieces and shape into smooth balls. Put one ball of dough into each flowerpot and cover with cling film. Leave in a warm place for 1 hour to rise.

**3** Heat oven to 200C/180C fan/gas 6. Remove the cling film from the pots and brush with a little milk or oil. Sprinkle with your choice of topping.

**4** Put the pots on a baking sheet in the oven and cook for 20–25 minutes until risen and golden. Leave to cool for 10 minutes before turning out and eating.

---

PER LOAF 434 kcals, protein 13g, carbs 74g, fat 8g, sat fat 1g, fibre 3g, sugar 4g, salt 1g

# Parmesan potato skins

*A great snack for a film night, served with a spicy salsa for dipping.*

**TAKES 1 HOUR 25 MINUTES**

● **SERVES 4**

4 large baking potatoes
1 tbsp olive oil
½ tsp cayenne pepper
½ tsp paprika
2 tbsp grated Parmesan (or vegetarian
    alternative)

**1** Heat oven to 180C/160C fan/gas 4.
Bake potatoes for 50–60 minutes.

**2** Leave to cool slightly, then halve them
and scrape out the middles, leaving
about 1cm/½in of potato in the skins.
Cut each skin into three and toss on a
baking sheet with oil, cayenne pepper,
paprika, ½ teaspoon salt and the
Parmesan. Bake for 10–15 minutes
more until crisp and golden.

PER SERVING 173 kcals, protein 5g, carbs 22g,
fat 5g, sat fat 2g, fibre 5g, sugar 1g, salt 0.8g

# Homemade Cajun tortilla chips

*Make your own tortilla chips to save time and calories! They taste better than the shop-bought varieties.*

**TAKES 20 MINUTES • SERVES 4**

2 tbsp oil
1 tbsp Cajun spice mix
8 plain tortillas

**1** Heat oven to 180C/160C fan/gas 4. Mix the oil with the Cajun spice mix. Brush the spiced oil over the tortillas, stacking the tortillas on top of each other as you go. Cut the stack into eight wedges. Separate the wedges, evenly spread them out on baking sheets and bake for 6–7 minutes until golden and crisp.

PER SERVING 385 kcals, protein 9g, carbs 71g, fat 7g, sat fat 1g, fibre 4g, sugar 2g, salt 0.9g

# Courgette fritters

*These fritters are a great snack served warm or cold, with a little sweet chilli sauce to dip them into.*

**TAKES 20 MINUTES** ● **SERVES 4**

50g/2oz plain flour
2 eggs
50ml/2fl oz milk
1 courgette, grated
1 tbsp oil
sweet chilli sauce, to serve

**1** Tip the flour into a bowl. Make a well in the centre, break in the eggs, then gradually whisk together adding the milk a little at a time to make a smooth batter. Stir in the courgette and season well.

**2** Heat the oil in a non-stick frying pan and add tablespoons of the fritter mixture. Cook for 2–3 minutes on each side until lightly golden. Serve with sweet chilli sauce.

PER SERVING 119 kcals, protein 6g, carbs 10g, fat 6g, sat fat 1g, fibre 1g, sugar 2g, salt 0.1g

# Spinach & feta falafel bites

*Keep a batch of these tasty bites in the fridge to curb those mid-afternoon cravings. They're perfect for dipping into low-fat tzatziki or houmous.*

**TAKES 55 MINUTES ● MAKES 30**

200g/7oz baby leaf spinach

400g can chickpeas, drained and rinsed

100g/4oz feta

2 tsp ground cumin

100g/4oz plain flour, plus extra for
    rolling

vegetable oil, for frying

low-fat tzatziki or houmous, to serve

**1** Pour a kettle of boiling water over the spinach in a colander. When cool enough to handle, squeeze out any water – do this really well or your falafels will be too soft. Pulse in a food processor with the drained chickpeas, feta, cumin and plain flour until just combined. Roll into tablespoon-sized balls with well-floured hands, then flatten into patties.
**2** Fry in batches in vegetable oil for 2–3 minutes each side, then leave to cool. Put on a baking sheet, cover with cling film and freeze. To serve, defrost in the fridge overnight and cook at 180C/160C fan/gas 4 for 5–10 minutes. Serve with tzatziki or houmous.

---

PER BITE 49 kcals, protein 2g, carbs 4g, fat 3g, sat fat 1g, fibre 1g, salt 0.16g

# Thai squash soup

*This warming, gently spiced soup is perfect on a cold day.*

**TAKES 35 MINUTES • SERVES 4**

1 onion, chopped

1 lemongrass stalk, bashed and
  shredded

1–2 red chillies, deseeded and roughly
  chopped

1 kg/2lb 4oz butternut squash, peeled
  and diced

juice 1 lime

125ml/4fl oz coconut milk

small bunch coriander, leaves picked

**1** Fry the onion, lemongrass and most of the chilli in a large pan with a splash of water for 2–3 minutes until softened – add more water if it starts to catch. Tip in the squash and stir. Cover with 1 litre/1¾ pints water, bring to the boil and simmer for 15 minutes until the squash is tender. Add the lime juice, remove from the heat and blitz with a hand blender until smooth.

**2** Pour in the coconut milk then return to the heat gently to warm through. Ladle into bowls and garnish with coriander and the remaining chilli.

PER SERVING 161 kcals, protein 4g, carbs 23g, fat 6g, sat fat 5g, fibre 5g, sugar 13g, salt none

# Spring minestrone

*If you want to bulk up this soup to a hearty stew, add some small pasta shapes to cook in the broth.*

**TAKES 40 MINUTES** • **SERVES 4**

3 tbsp olive oil

2 leeks, finely sliced

2 celery sticks, finely chopped

2 courgettes, quartered lengthways then sliced

4 garlic cloves, finely chopped

1 litre/1¾ pints vegetable stock

250g/9oz asparagus, woody ends removed, chopped

100g/4oz peas, fresh or frozen

200g/7oz broad beans, double-podded, if you have time

small bunch basil, most torn, some leaves left whole to scatter

crusty bread, to serve

**1** Heat the oil in a large pan, add the leeks and celery, and cook for 8 minutes until soft. Add the courgettes and garlic. Cook gently for 5 minutes more.

**2** Pour in the stock and simmer, covered, for 10 minutes. Add the asparagus, peas and broad beans, and cook for a further 4 minutes, until just cooked through. Stir in the torn basil and season well. Scatter with a few whole basil leaves and serve with crusty bread.

PER SERVING 188 kcals, protein 10g, carbs 13g, fat 11g, sat fat 2g, fibre 11g, sugar 7g, salt 0.7g

# Courgette & tomato soup

*Use up a garden glut of veggies in this simple but tasty low-fat soup.*

**TAKES 45 MINUTES** ● **SERVES 8**

1 tbsp butter
2 onions, chopped
1kg/2lb 4oz courgettes, sliced
1kg/2lb 4oz tomatoes, chopped
2 tbsp plain flour
½ tsp turmeric powder
2 litres/3½ pints chicken or vegetable
    stock from cubes
crusty bread, to serve (optional)

**1** Melt the butter in a large pan, add the onions and courgettes, and cook for 5 minutes on a medium heat, stirring occasionally.

**2** Add the tomatoes and flour. Cook for a couple of minutes, stirring to stop the flour becoming lumpy. Add the turmeric and stock, cover and simmer for 30 minutes.

**3** Purée with a stick blender, then sieve if you want a really smooth texture. Serve hot with crusty bread, if you like, or chill, then freeze for up to 2 months.

---

PER SERVING 90 kcals, protein 4g, carbs 12g, fat 3g, sat fat 1g, fibre 4g, sugar 8g, salt 0.8g

# Mexican chicken & wild rice soup

*Take this soup to work in a thermos or sealed container and simply pop it in the microwave for a speedy and substantial lunch.*

**TAKES 30 MINUTES • SERVES 4**

1 tsp olive oil

1 onion, finely chopped

1 green pepper, deseeded and diced

200g/7oz sweetcorn, frozen or from a can

1–2 tbsp chipotle paste (we used Discovery)

250g pouch ready-cooked long grain and wild rice mix (we used Uncle Ben's)

400g can black beans in water, drained and rinsed

1.3 litres/2¼ pints low-sodium chicken stock

2 cooked skinless chicken breasts, shredded

small bunch coriander, chopped

low-fat soured cream and reduced-fat guacamole, to serve (optional)

**1** Heat the oil in a large non-stick pan and gently cook the onion for 5 minutes. Throw in the pepper and cook for 2 minutes more, then add the sweetcorn, chipotle paste and rice. Stir well and cook for 1–2 minutes.

**2** Add the black beans and the stock. Bring to the boil, turn down to a simmer, then add half the chicken and coriander. Cool for 2–3 minutes, then ladle into four bowls.

**3** Scatter over the rest of the chicken and coriander. Serve with a dollop each of guacamole and soured cream on top, if you like.

---

PER SERVING 347 kcals, protein 29g, carbs 45g, fat 7g, sat fat 1g, fibre 5g, sugar 5g, salt 0.48g

# Chicken, sweetcorn & noodle soup

*Classic chicken noodle soup is always a winner. Kids will love the added nuggets of fresh sweetcorn.*

**TAKES 1½ HOURS ● SERVES 8**

1.3kg/3lb chicken
2 large carrots, chopped
2 large leeks, trimmed and finely sliced
2 corn on the cobs, kernels cut off
200g/7oz vermicelli noodles
small bunch parsley, finely chopped,
   to garnish

**FOR THE STOCK**

2 onions, quartered
1 leek, cut into chunks
2 carrots, thickly sliced
2 bay leaves
6 black peppercorns
few parsley stalks
4 celery sticks, roughly chopped
2 tbsp vegetable bouillon or
   1 vegetable stock cube

**1** Put all the stock ingredients and the chicken in a very large pan, then cover everything with about 3 litres/5¼ pints cold water. Bring to the boil, then lower to a simmer for 1–1½ hours, until the chicken is cooked through. Skim off any froth every 20 minutes or so.

**2** Remove the chicken to a plate to cool. Strain the stock through a sieve, skimming off as much fat as you can.

**3** Rinse out the pan and put the stock back in, then simmer on a high heat until reduced a little – you need about 2 litres/3½ pints in total. Add the carrots and leeks, then simmer for 10 minutes.

**4** Meanwhile, shred the meat from the chicken, discarding the skin and bones. Add to the pan with the sweetcorn. Add the vermicelli noodles, unless you want to freeze the soup, and simmer for about 7 minutes more, until the corn and pasta are cooked. Ladle into bowls, sprinkled with the parsley.

---

PER SERVING 288 kcals, protein 25g, carbs 28g, fat 9g, sat fat 3g, fibre 2g, sugar 5g, salt 0.71g

# Chicken–chickpea salad with curry yogurt dressing

*Chickpeas make for a really substantial salad.*

**TAKES 30 MINUTES • SERVES 2**

2 chicken breasts
200ml/7fl oz 0% fat Greek yogurt
2 tsp mild curry powder
juice ½ lemon
small handful mint leaves, most
    chopped, some left whole
400g can chickpeas, drained and rinsed
100g/4oz cherry tomatoes, quartered
1 small red onion, chopped
1 tbsp peanuts, crushed

**1** Bring a pan of water to the boil. Add the chicken breasts and some salt, then put on the lid. Turn off the heat and leave for 15 minutes until cooked through. Drain, then shred the chicken.
**2** In a small bowl, mix the yogurt, curry powder, lemon juice, chopped mint and some seasoning to make a dressing.
**3** Toss the chicken and chickpeas with half the dressing, and season. Arrange on two plates and scatter over the tomatoes, onion, whole mint leaves and peanuts. Drizzle the extra dressing over the top.

PER SERVING 406 kcals, protein 50g, carbs 32g, fat 7g, sat fat 1g, fibre 7g, sugar 8g, salt 1.3g

# Spicy chicken & bean wrap

*Use up leftover roast chicken in this tasty lunchtime treat.*

**TAKES 5 MINUTES ● MAKES 1**

1 large flour tortilla wrap

handful leftover cooked chicken, shredded

4 tbsp black beans or kidney beans, drained and rinsed

2 tbsp spicy salsa from a jar

4 slices pickled jalapeño peppers (or a good splash Tabasco sauce)

3 cherry tomatoes, halved

handful rocket or spinach leaves

**1** Warm the tortilla in the microwave for 10 seconds; this will soften it, which makes it easier to roll. Put the chicken and beans along the middle. Season, then spoon over the salsa and scatter with peppers or Tabasco. Lay the tomatoes and leaves on top. Bring the bottom of the tortilla up over the filling. Fold the sides in, then roll into a tight wrap. Pack up tightly to keep it together.

PER WRAP 348 kcals, protein 29g, carbs 47g, fat 6g, sat fat 1g, fibre 6g, sugar 5g, salt 1.05g

# Stuffed jackets

*Get the kids to help you make these easy, cheesy stuffed jackets. You can add whatever fillings you like.*

**TAKES 1 HOUR 35 MINUTES**

● **SERVES 4**

4 medium potatoes

85g/3oz strong Cheddar, grated, plus extra for topping

100g/4oz sweetcorn

100g/4oz mixed peppers, deseeded and diced

small handful fresh herbs, such as oregano, basil, coriander, dill or thyme, leaves picked

**1** Heat oven to 200C/180C fan/gas 6 and bake the potatoes for about 1 hour until cooked and the skins are crispy. Leave to cool completely. This can be done up to 2 days ahead.

**2** To stuff the jacket potatoes, heat the oven to 200C/180C fan/gas 6. Cut the potatoes in half. Using a spoon, scoop out the middle of the potato, leaving the skin unbroken. Put the scooped potato into a mixing bowl.

**3** Using the fork, mash the potato until there are no lumps. Add the cheese, sweetcorn, peppers and herbs, and mix well.

**4** Scoop the mixture back into the potato skins. Sprinkle with a little extra grated cheese and put on a baking sheet. Using oven gloves, put the tin in the oven and bake for 10–15 minutes until golden.

---

PER SERVING 238 kcals, protein 10g, carbs 30g, fat 9g, sat fat 5g, fibre 3g, sugar 3g, salt 0.4g

# Open prawn-cocktail sandwich

*You'll love this lighter version of a classic prawn cocktail.*

**TAKES 15 MINUTES • MAKES 2**

2 tbsp extra-light mayonnaise

1 tbsp reduced-sugar ketchup

2 tbsp chopped dill

1 lemon, cut into 8 wedges

100g pack cooked peeled North
   Atlantic prawns

½ cucumber, deseeded and diced

2 handfuls cherry tomatoes, halved

2 slices wholemeal bread

20g bag rocket leaves

**1** Make the dressing in a medium bowl. Mix the mayonnaise, ketchup, half the dill, the juice from 4 of the lemon wedges and some seasoning. Toss in the prawns, cucumber and tomatoes.

**2** Arrange the bread on two plates, top each with rocket leaves and pile on the prawn filling. Scatter with the remaining dill and serve with the rest of the lemon wedges, for squeezing over.

PER SANDWICH 173 kcals, protein 17g, carbs 22g, fat 3g, sat fat none, fibre 3g, sugar 7g, salt 1.5g

# Mexican rice & bean salad

*This salad would also work well alongside a Mexican-style supper with tacos or fajitas.*

**TAKES 35 MINUTES • SERVES 4**

175g/6oz basmati and wild rice mix
400g can mixed bean salad, drained
   and rinsed
bunch spring onions, chopped
1 red pepper, deseeded and chopped
1 avocado, chopped
juice 1 lime, plus wedges to serve
1 tbsp Cajun spice mix
small bunch coriander, chopped

**1** Cook the rice according to the pack instructions. Drain, then cool under cold running water until completely cold. Stir in the beans, onions, pepper and avocado.
**2** Mix the lime juice with the Cajun spice mix and some freshly ground black pepper. Pour over the rice mix, stir in the coriander and serve with extra lime wedges.

PER SERVING 326 kcals, protein 11g, carbs 44g, fat 10g, sat fat 2g, fibre 6g, sugar 4g, salt none

# Pesto-chicken pasta salad

*Most kids love pesto, and you may even get some veggies down them with this pesto–pasta salad.*

**TAKES 30 MINUTES ● SERVES 1**
85g/3oz pasta shapes
½ red pepper, deseeded and chopped
handful cherry tomatoes, halved
1 cooked chicken breast
1 tbsp basil pesto
2 tbsp low-fat crème fraîche

**1** Cook the pasta according to the pack instructions.
**2** Meanwhile, mix the red pepper with the cherry tomatoes and chicken. Combine the pesto and crème fraîche in a small bowl. Drain the pasta, then stir through the pesto mix. Toss through the veg and chicken, and eat immediately, or pack into a container for lunch.

PER SERVING 600 kcals, protein 47g, carbs 68g, fat 15g, sat fat 4g, fibre 4g, sugar 7g, salt 0.3g

# Beetroot, carrot & chickpea pittas with yogurt dressing

*A new way to fill pitta bread. Grate the veggies to make these pitta pockets more appealing to kids.*

**TAKES 10 MINUTES ● SERVES 2**

2 large wholemeal pitta breads
1 cooked beetroot, grated
1 small carrot, grated
few mint leaves
200g/7oz cooked chickpeas, drained
    and rinsed
1 tsp harissa paste
2 tbsp 0% fat Greek yogurt

**1** Split the pittas in half. In a bowl, mix together the beetroot, carrot, mint and chickpeas, then season. Swirl the harissa into the yogurt and spread inside the pittas. Fill with the beetroot mixture and wrap up ready for lunch or eat straight away. Great served with a healthy shake.

PER SERVING 332 kcals, protein 17g, carbs 55g, fat 3g, sat fat 1g, fibre 9g, sugar 9g, salt 1.5g

# Rainbow tomato salad

*Simple, yet stunning. Serve with cold sliced meat and bread for the perfect lunch.*

**TAKES 10 MINUTES ● SERVES 6**

1 kg/2lb 4oz ripe tomatoes of various colours, shapes and sizes, at room temperature
sea salt, to season
2 tbsp balsamic vinegar
drizzle extra-virgin olive oil
handful basil leaves

**1** Slice the tomatoes and arrange on a platter, then season with a small pinch of sea salt and some freshly ground black pepper. Drizzle over the vinegar and oil, and scatter over the basil to serve.

PER SERVING 35 kcals, protein 1g, carbs 5g, fat 1g, sat fat none, fibre 2g, sugar 5g, salt 1.5g

# Salmon & chive bagel topper

*Salmon makes a great healthy lunch, packed full of essential nutrients. Take this topper to work in a plastic tub and spread on bagels for lunch.*

**TAKES 10 MINUTES • SERVES 4**

1 cooked salmon fillet (about 100g/4oz in total)
200g/7oz reduced-fat soft cheese
zest and juice ½ lemon
2 tbsp snipped chives
4 multiseed bagels, split in half
4 small handfuls watercress

**1** Flake the salmon into a bowl. Add the cheese, lemon zest and juice, chives and plenty of freshly ground black pepper. Mash everything together with a fork, then keep chilled until lunchtime.
**2** Lightly toast the bagel halves, then spread with the salmon mixture and top each with a handful of watercress. Eat straight away.

PER SERVING 368 kcals, protein 24g, carbs 39g, fat 11g, sat fat 4g, fibre 6g, sugar 6g, salt 1.5g

# Chicken, carrot & avocado rolls

*Bite-sized roll-ups, perfect for popping into lunchboxes.*

**TAKES 15 MINUTES** ● **SERVES 3**

75g/2½oz low-fat soft cheese
3 flour tortillas
1 cooked skinless chicken breast,
  coarsely shredded
1 large carrot, grated or shredded
1 large avocado, stoned and sliced
handful rocket leaves

**1** Spread the cheese over the tortillas and top with the chicken, carrot, avocado and rocket.

**2** Tightly roll up each tortilla. Wrap tightly in cling film, twisting the ends firmly to seal, and chill until ready to eat.

---

PER SERVING 352 kcals, protein 20g, carbs 29g, fat 17g, sat fat 5g, fibre 6g, sugar 6g, salt 0.7g

# Crab & avocado wrap

*Tinned crab is low in fat and available in most supermarkets. If you can find fresh crab it will make this wrap even more special.*

**TAKES 10 MINUTES • MAKES 2**

1 small red onion, sliced into thin rings
juice 2 limes, plus wedges to squeeze over
pinch caster sugar
170g can white crabmeat in brine, drained
2 spring onions, finely sliced
1 red chilli, deseeded and chopped
1 really ripe avocado, chopped
1 small garlic clove, crushed
2 corn tortillas
handful mixed salad leaves

**1** Put the onion in a bowl and cover with half the lime juice and a good pinch each of sugar and salt. Leave to soften while you get everything else ready.

**2** Mix together the crabmeat, spring onions and half the chilli. Season with freshly ground black pepper and set aside. Mash the avocado with the remaining lime juice, the garlic and some seasoning. You can leave it quite chunky or mash it until smooth. Stir in the rest of the chilli.

**3** Bend each tortilla in half and toast in a toaster for 1 minute. Put on two plates and top with the salad leaves, then the mashed avocado. Finish with the crabmeat mix and top with the marinated red-onion rings. Serve with lime wedges for squeezing over.

PER WRAP 394 kcals, protein 22g, carbs 27g, fat 19g, sat fat 5g, fibre 6g, sugar 5g, salt 1.1g

# Spicy-tuna quinoa salad

*Protein-packed quinoa is a great alternative to pasta or rice. If you don't like it spicy, leave out the chilli.*

**TAKES 20 MINUTES** • **SERVES 4**

1 onion, sliced

350g/12oz red peppers, deseeded and sliced

1 tbsp olive oil

1 red chilli, deseeded and finely chopped

225g pouch ready-to-eat quinoa

350g/12oz cherry tomatoes, halved

handful pitted black olives, chopped

225g jar albacore tuna in olive oil, drained (oil reserved) and flaked

**1** Fry the onion and peppers in the oil until soft. Add the chilli and cool slightly.

**2** Mix the quinoa, onion mixture, cherry tomatoes, olives and tuna together. Divide among four plates, pour over a little of the oil from the tuna jar, season and serve.

---

PER SERVING 298 kcals, protein 17g, carbs 28g, fat 13g, sat fat 2g, fibre 7g, sugar 10g, salt 0.7g

# Charred pepper, bulghar & aubergine salad

*This salad makes a great side dish for a barbecue; if the barbecue is lit, cook the vegetables on it instead of on the grill for a lovely smoky flavour.*

**TAKES 20 MINUTES • SERVES 4**

175g/6oz bulghar wheat
2 tbsp sundried tomato paste
4 baby aubergines, each sliced
    lengthways into 3
1 red pepper, deseeded and sliced
    lengthways into 1cm/½in pieces
2 tsp olive oil
handful basil leaves

**1** Prepare the bulghar according to the pack instructions. Tip into a large bowl and stir through the tomato paste; season.

**2** Heat a griddle pan to high. Drizzle the aubergines and red pepper with the oil, and cook for 5 minutes on each side until lightly charred.

**3** Stir the aubergines and red pepper into the bulghar mixture, then season and stir through the basil.

PER SERVING 198 kcals, protein 6g, carbs 38g, fat 3g, sat fat none, fibre 6g, sugar 6g, salt 0.2g

# Crunchy prawn-noodle salad

*A light and zesty noodle salad is a great alternative to a soggy sandwich. You can swap the prawns for shredded chicken, if you like.*

**TAKES 15 MINUTES • SERVES 2**

100g/4oz rice noodles

2 small carrots, cut into thin matchsticks

2 spring onions, thinly sliced

small handful each coriander and mint leaves, chopped

140g/5oz cooked peeled prawns in chilli, lime and coriander (we used Waitrose)

1 tsp reduced-salt soy sauce

½ tsp Thai fish sauce

2 tsp light soft brown sugar

zest and juice 1 lime

**1** Soak the noodles in boiling water according to the pack instructions. Drain and run under cold water until cool, then drain well again. Mix the noodles with the carrots, spring onions, coriander, mint and prawns.

**2** In a small bowl, whisk the remaining ingredients together, pour over the noodle salad and toss well to coat. Store in containers until ready to eat.

PER SERVING 314 kcals, protein 18g, carbs 51g, fat 2g, sat fat 0.3g, fibre 4g, sugar 12g, salt 1.4g

# Grilled salmon tacos with chipotle-lime yogurt

*The spiced salmon for these tacos is grilled, making them a much healthier alternative to classic minced–beef tacos.*

**TAKES 25 MINUTES • SERVES 4**

1 tsp garlic salt
2 tbsp smoked paprika
good pinch sugar
500g/1lb 2oz salmon fillets
200ml/7fl oz fat-free yogurt
1 tbsp chipotle paste or hot chilli sauce
juice 1 lime

**TO SERVE**

8 small soft flour tortillas, warmed
¼ small green cabbage, finely shredded
small bunch coriander, picked into
    sprigs
few pickled jalapeño chillies, sliced
lime wedges, to squeeze over
hot chilli sauce, to taste (optional)

**1** Rub the garlic salt, paprika, sugar and some seasoning into the flesh of the salmon fillets. Heat grill to high.

**2** Mix the yogurt, chipotle paste or chilli sauce and lime juice together in a bowl with some seasoning, and set aside. Put the salmon on a baking sheet lined with foil and grill, skin-side down, for 7–8 minutes until cooked through. Remove from the grill and carefully peel off and discard the skin.

**3** Flake the salmon into large chunks and serve with the warmed tortillas, chipotle yogurt, shredded cabbage, coriander, jalapeños and lime wedges. Add a shake of hot sauce, if you like it spicy.

PER SERVING 297 kcals, protein 33g, carbs 8g, fat 15g, sat fat 3g, fibre 5g, sugar 7g, salt 1.5g

# Baked turkey meatballs with broccoli & crispy potatoes

*Serve these lighter turkey meatballs with crispy potatoes, mash or spaghetti.*

**TAKES 55 MINUTES ● SERVES 4**

1 onion, grated
1 large carrot, grated
3 garlic cloves, crushed
1 tbsp rosemary leaves, chopped
350g pack minced turkey
4 large potatoes, skin on and cut into
  small cubes
1 tbsp olive oil
400g can cherry tomatoes
2 tbsp grated Parmesan
350g/12oz thin-stemmed broccoli
bunch basil leaves, shredded
crispy potatoes and broccoli, to serve

**1** Heat oven to 220C/200C fan/gas 7. In a large bowl, combine the onion, carrot, half the garlic and half the rosemary with the turkey and some seasoning. Shape into 16 meatballs and put on a small baking sheet. Toss the potatoes with the remaining garlic, rosemary and the oil, put on another baking sheet, then cook both for 20 minutes, with the potatoes on the top shelf.

**2** After 20 minutes, drain the juices off the meatballs, pour the cherry tomatoes over, sprinkle with the Parmesan and season. Toss the potatoes and swap them to the bottom shelf. Cook for another 20 minutes until the potatoes are golden and crisp and the meatball sauce is bubbling.

**3** When the potatoes and meatballs are almost done, cook the broccoli for 3–4 minutes, until tender. Sprinkle the basil on top of the meatballs and serve with the crispy potatoes and broccoli.

PER SERVING 279 kcals, protein 31g, carbs 22g, fat 7g, sat fat 2g, fibre 5g, sugar 8g, salt 0.4g

# Cod with bacon, lettuce & peas

*This French bistro classic makes an easy one-pot supper. Serve simply with brown bread to soak up the juices.*

**TAKES 20 MINUTES • SERVES 2**

2 tsp sunflower oil

2 rashers rindless smoked streaky bacon, cut into small pieces

1 long shallot or small onion, very finely sliced

1 garlic clove, crushed

2 × 140g/5oz thick skinless cod fillets

140g/5oz frozen peas

200ml/7fl oz chicken stock, fresh or made with ½ low-sodium stock cube

2 Little Gem lettuces, thickly shredded

2 tbsp half-fat crème fraîche

2 thick slices crusty wholegrain bread, to serve

**1** Heat the sunflower oil in a medium non-stick frying pan. Add the bacon, shallot or onion and garlic. Cook gently, stirring, for 2 minutes, then push to one side of the pan.

**2** Season the cod with ground black pepper. Fry in the pan for 2 minutes, then turn over. Add the peas and stock, and bring to a simmer. Cook over a medium heat for a further 2 minutes, then add the lettuce and crème fraîche. Cook for a couple of minutes more, stirring the vegetables occasionally, until the fish is just cooked and the lettuce has wilted. Serve with bread to mop up the broth.

PER SERVING 312 kcals, protein 38g, carbs 9g, fat 14g, sat fat 5g, fibre 5g, sugar 5g, salt 1.1g

# Prawn fajitas with avocado cream

*Classic Mexican flavours of chilli, lime and coriander infuse the prawns in these tasty tortilla wraps.*

**TAKES 25 MINUTES** • **SERVES 2**

juice 2 limes, plus wedges to squeeze over

1 red chilli, deseeded and chopped

2 garlic cloves, crushed

small bunch coriander, chopped

225g/8oz large raw peeled prawns

1 avocado, chopped

1 heaped tbsp soured cream, plus extra to serve

1 tbsp olive oil

1 red pepper, deseeded and sliced

4 flour tortillas and a good handful mixed salad leaves, to serve (optional)

**1** Mix half the lime juice, half the chilli, half the garlic and half the coriander with some seasoning in a shallow dish. Add the prawns and mix to coat them all. Leave to marinate while you prepare the avocado.

**2** Roughly chop the avocado and pop it in a small food processor with the remaining lime juice, chilli, garlic, the soured cream and some seasoning. Whizz until smooth, then stir in the remaining coriander. (You could also use a stick blender for this.)

**3** Heat the oil in a frying pan and cook the pepper for a few minutes, until starting to soften. Add the prawns and fry, in a single layer, for 1–2 minutes each side – you will know they are cooked when they turn pink and feel firm to the touch. Serve in warm tortillas with salad leaves, if you like, alongside the avocado cream, extra soured cream and some lime wedges.

PER SERVING 320 kcals, protein 23g, carbs 8g, fat 22g, sat fat 5g, fibre 5g, sugar 6g, salt 0.6g

# Pollack, beetroot & potato traybake

*This tasty fish dish is all cooked in one pan, to save on the washing up!*

**TAKES 55 MINUTES • SERVES 4**

4 small potatoes, sliced
1 tbsp olive oil
2 tsp fennel seeds, lightly crushed
4 beetroot, peeled and cut into wedges
4 pollack fillets
zest ½ lemon
4 tbsp low-fat crème fraîche
small handful basil leaves, roughly
    chopped, to garnish

**1** Heat oven to 200C/180C fan/gas 6. Put the potatoes in a large baking tin and toss with the oil and fennel seeds. Season, arrange in a single layer, then bake for 20 minutes until softened and starting to crisp.

**2** Turn the potatoes over and add the beetroot, season and return to the oven for 15 minutes. Put the fish in the centre, season well and rub over a little oil from the tin. Return to the oven for 10 minutes more.

**3** Meanwhile, sprinkle the lemon zest over the crème fraîche with a good grind of black pepper. To serve, scatter the fish with basil and dollop with some of the lemony crème fraîche.

PER SERVING 292 kcals, protein 26g, carbs 31g, fat 7g, sat fat 3g, fibre 3g, sugar 3g, salt 0.4g

# Prawn skewers with rice salad

*You'll find frozen soya beans in most supermarkets. Save any leftover skewers and salad for lunch the next day.*

**TAKES 40 MINUTES** ● **SERVES 4**

200g/7oz brown basmati rice
175g/6oz mangetout
200g/7oz frozen soy beans
1½ tbsp sesame oil
4 spring onions, finely sliced
large handful coriander, roughly
    chopped
1 green chilli, deseeded and
    finely diced

**FOR THE SKEWERS**

400g/14oz raw large peeled prawns
3 tbsp sweet miso paste (find this with
    the Japanese ingredients. We used
    Clearspring white miso)
2 tsp soy sauce
2 tsp Japanese rice vinegar
2 tsp soft brown sugar

**1** Put the brown rice in a pan with lots of cold water. Bring to the boil and simmer for 20–25 minutes or until tender. Meanwhile, soak eight wooden skewers in some cold water (to prevent them burning). Add the mangetout and soy beans to the rice for the final 5 minutes of cooking. Rinse under cold water, draining thoroughly.

**2** Toss the rice and veg with the sesame oil and mix in a large bowl with the spring onions, coriander, chilli and some seasoning.

**3** Heat a grill. Put the skewer ingredients in a bowl with a few grinds of black pepper. Give everything a good stir, making sure the prawns are well coated. Thread prawns on to the skewers and lay on a baking sheet. Grill for a couple of minutes on each side, until the prawns are cooked through. Serve with the rice salad and drizzle over any of the cooking juices.

---

PER SERVING 410 kcals, protein 32g, carbs 47g, fat 10g, sat fat 2g, fibre 7g, sugar 8g, salt 1.5g

# More veg, less meat bolognese

*This simple pasta dish is a great way to sneak extra veggies on to a kid's plate.*

**TAKES 20 MINUTES • SERVES 4**

2 tbsp olive oil
2 onions, finely chopped
3 carrots, finely chopped
4 celery sticks, finely chopped
2 courgettes, cut into small cubes
4 garlic cloves, finely chopped
250g pack minced beef
1 heaped tbsp tomato purée
400g can chopped tomatoes
400g/14oz fettuccine
200g/7oz peas, frozen or fresh
handful parsley, roughly chopped

**1** Heat the oil in large deep frying pan. Add the onions, carrots, celery, courgettes and garlic. Cook for about 10 minutes or until soft, adding a few splashes of water if the mixture begins to stick. Turn up the heat and add the mince. Fry for a few minutes more, breaking up the mince with the back of a spoon. Stir in the tomato purée, pour over the chopped tomatoes and add a can of water. Simmer for 15 minutes until the sauce is thick, then season.

**2** Meanwhile, cook the fettuccine according to the pack instructions. Drain.

**3** Tip the peas into the sauce and simmer for 2 minutes more until tender. Stir through the drained pasta and parsley, then serve.

PER SERVING 474 kcals, protein 25g, carbs 58g, fat 16g, sat fat 4g, fibre 8g, sugar 14g, salt 0.3g

# Chicken arrabiata

*A spicy chicken dish, perfect for a Friday-night supper for friends or family.*

**TAKES ¼ HOUR • SERVES 6**

3 tbsp olive oil
2 onions, halved and sliced
1 garlic bulb, separated into cloves
2 red chillies, deseeded and sliced
350ml/12fl oz red wine
350ml/12fl oz chicken stock
600g/1lb 5oz tomatoes, finely chopped
3 tbsp tomato purée
2 tsp chopped thyme
6 skinless chicken legs
chopped parsley, to garnish (optional)
pasta or mash, to serve

**1** Heat the olive oil in a large heavy-based pan. Add the onions and garlic cloves. Fry, stirring frequently, for 10 minutes, adding the chillies for the final minute.

**2** Pour in the wine, turn up the heat and allow it to bubble for 1 minute to cook off the alcohol. Stir in the stock, tomatoes, tomato purée and thyme with some seasoning. Add the chicken legs, pushing them under the liquid, then part-cover the pan and leave to simmer gently for 45 minutes.

**3** Remove the lid and cook for a further 15 minutes until the chicken is tender and the sauce has reduced a little. Serve scattered with parsley, if you like, and pasta or mash.

PER SERVING 327 kcals, protein 35g, carbs 9g, fat 13g, sat fat 3g, fibre 3g, sugar 7g, salt 0.5g

# Turkey-chilli jacket potatoes

*Keep a batch of this turkey chilli in the freezer for a quick meal any time.*

**TAKES 55 MINUTES • MAKES 4**

4 large baking potatoes
1 tbsp olive oil
1 onion, chopped
1 garlic clove, crushed
300g/10oz minced turkey
1 tbsp smoked paprika
1 tbsp ground cumin
1 tbsp cider vinegar
1 tbsp light soft brown sugar
350ml/12fl oz passata
reduced-fat Red Leicester, grated,
　to sprinkle
4 spring onions, chopped, to garnish

**1** Heat oven to 200C/180C fan/gas 6. Use a fork to prick the potatoes all over. Rub with a little of the oil and bake for 45 minutes until tender.

**2** Meanwhile, make the chilli. Heat the remaining oil in a large frying pan over a medium heat. Add the onion, garlic and some seasoning, and cook for 5 minutes until soft. Add the turkey mince and season again, then increase the heat and break up the mince with the back of your spoon. When it's cooked through, add the spices, vinegar, sugar and passata. Reduce to a simmer and cook for 10 minutes or until the liquid has reduced.

**3** Cut a cross in the top of each potato and spoon in the chilli. Serve each potato sprinkled with cheese and spring onions.

PER POTATO 410 kcals, protein 30g, carbs 61g, fat 5g, sat fat 1g, fibre 7g, sugar 13g, salt 0.1g

# Pasta salad with tuna, capers & balsamic dressing

*Kids love tuna pasta, so try them on this updated healthier version.*

**TAKES 20 MINUTES ● SERVES 4**

350g/12oz orecchiette
225g jar tuna in spring water, drained and flaked
1 tbsp capers, drained
10 peppadew peppers from a jar, drained and chopped
1 celery heart, sliced
140g/5oz yellow, red or a mixture of cherry tomatoes, halved
75ml/2½fl oz balsamic vinegar
3 tbsp extra-virgin olive oil
100g bag rocket leaves
good handful basil leaves, to garnish

**1** Cook the pasta according to the pack instructions, then drain and rinse in cold water. After draining again, transfer to a large bowl.
**2** Add the remaining ingredients to the pasta, except the basil, season well, and toss to combine. Scatter with the basil and serve.

PER SERVING 527 kcals, protein 24g, carbs 82g, fat 10g, sat fat 2g, fibre 3g, sugar 14g, salt 0.6g

# Barley, chicken & mushroom risotto

*Pearl barley gives this risotto a lovely nutty bite – try using it in other risottos too.*

**TAKES 1 HOUR • SERVES 4**

1 tbsp butter
1 tbsp olive oil
2 large shallots, finely sliced
1 garlic clove, chopped
3 boneless, skinless chicken breasts,
   cut into chunky pieces
300g/10oz pearl barley
250ml/9fl oz white wine
400g/14oz mixed wild and chestnut
   mushrooms, chopped
1 tbsp thyme leaves
1 litre/1¾ pints hot chicken stock
3 tbsp grated Parmesan
snipped chives and Parmesan shavings,
   to garnish (optional)

**1** In a large, heavy pan, heat the butter and oil. Sauté the shallots and garlic with some seasoning for 5 minutes, then stir in the chicken and cook for 2 minutes.
**2** Add the barley and cook for 1 minute. Pour in the wine and stir until it is absorbed. Add the mushrooms and thyme, then pour over three-quarters of the stock. Cook for 40 minutes on a low simmer until the barley is tender, stirring occasionally and topping up with the remaining stock if it looks dry. Remove from the heat and stir in the grated Parmesan. Serve immediately, with chives and Parmesan shavings scattered over, if you like.

PER SERVING 564 kcals, protein 42g, carbs 61g, fat 12g, sat fat 5g, fibre 3g, sugar 3g, salt 1.1g

# Lentil lasagne

*This pasta bake is vegan friendly – it uses soya milk and cauliflower purée for the white sauce and lentils for the filling.*

**TAKES 1½ HOURS ● SERVES 4**

1 tbsp olive oil
1 onion, chopped
1 carrot, chopped
1 celery stick, chopped
1 garlic clove, crushed
2 × 400g cans lentils, drained and
   rinsed
1 tbsp cornflour
400g can chopped tomatoes
1 tsp mushroom ketchup
1 tsp chopped oregano leaves or
   1 tsp dried
1 tsp vegetable stock powder
2 cauliflower heads, broken into florets
2 tbsp unsweetened soya milk
pinch freshly grated nutmeg
9 dried egg-free lasagne sheets

**1** Heat the oil in a pan. Add the onion, carrot and celery. Gently cook for 10–15 minutes. Add the garlic, cook for a few minutes, then add the lentils and cornflour.
**2** Add the tomatoes plus a canful of water, the mushroom ketchup, oregano, stock powder and some seasoning. Simmer for 15 minutes.
**3** Cook the cauliflower in a pan of boiling water for 10 minutes. Drain, then purée with the soya milk using a hand blender. Season and add the nutmeg.
**4** Heat oven to 180C/160C fan/gas 4. Spread a third of the lentil mixture over the base of a baking dish, about 20cm × 30cm. Cover with a layer of lasagne. Add another third of the lentil mixture, then spread a third of the cauliflower purée on top, followed by a layer of pasta. Top with the last third of lentils and lasagne, and remaining purée.
**5** Cover loosely with foil and bake for 35–45 minutes (remove the foil for the final 10 minutes).

PER SERVING 378 kcals, protein 19g, carbs 63g, fat 6g, sat fat 1g, fibre 10g, sugar 11g, salt 0.3g

# Cherry tomato, kale & ricotta-pesto pasta

*Kale is packed full of superfood goodness, and this pasta dish is a great way to get it into your diet.*

**TAKES 25 MINUTES • SERVES 4**

2 tbsp olive oil
3 garlic cloves, chopped
1 tsp crushed chilli flakes
2 × 400g cans cherry tomatoes
500g/1lb 2oz penne
200g/7oz kale, chopped
4 tbsp ricotta
4 tbsp fresh pesto
Parmesan, to garnish (optional)

**1** Heat the oil in a large pan, add the garlic and cook for 2 minutes until golden. Add the chilli flakes and tomatoes, season well, and simmer for 15 minutes until the sauce is thick and reduced.

**2** While the sauce is cooking, cook the pasta according to the pack instructions – add the kale for the final 2 minutes of cooking. Drain well and stir into the sauce, then divide among four bowls. Top each with a tablespoon of ricotta and pesto plus shavings of Parmesan, if you like.

PER SERVING 641 kcals, protein 24g, carbs 99g, fat 17g, sat fat 2g, fibre 7g, sugar 9g, salt 0.4g

# Raid-the-cupboard tuna sweetcorn cakes

*Tinned fish is a life saver when you need to rustle up a healthy, budget-friendly supper in a hurry.*

**TAKES 40 MINUTES** ● **SERVES 4**

450g/1lb potatoes, quartered
2 tbsp mayonnaise, plus extra to serve
2 × 185g cans tuna, drained
198g can sweetcorn, drained
small bunch chives, snipped, or 1 tsp
    dried parsley
2 eggs, beaten
100g/4oz dried breadcrumbs
sunflower oil, for frying
salad and your favourite dressing,
    to serve

**1** Cook the potatoes in boiling salted water until really tender. Drain and allow to steam-dry in a colander. Tip into a bowl, season and mash. Stir in the mayonnaise, tuna, sweetcorn and chives or parsley. Shape into four cakes and chill until cold and firm.

**2** Dip each cake into the egg, letting the excess drip off, then coat in the breadcrumbs. Chill for 15 minutes.

**3** Heat a little of the oil in a pan and gently fry the cakes for 2–3 minutes on each side until golden. You may need to do this in batches – keep warm in a low oven. Serve with extra mayonnaise and dressed salad leaves.

PER CAKE 467 kcals, protein 27g, carbs 42g, fat 22g, sat fat 3g, fibre 3g, sugar 4g, salt 1.3g

# Sticky cod with celeriac-parsley mash

*Use celeriac instead of potatoes for a chunky, healthy mash.*

**TAKES 35 MINUTES • SERVES 4**

2 tbsp extra-virgin olive oil
4 × 120g/4½oz pieces cod
little plain flour, for dusting
2 garlic cloves, chopped
1 tsp crushed chilli flakes
3 tbsp sherry vinegar
1 tbsp soft brown sugar
lemon wedges, to squeeze over

**FOR THE MASH**

1 large head celeriac, peeled and
    cubed (about 500g/1lb 2oz in total)
2 tbsp butter
big handful parsley, finely chopped

**1** To make the mash, boil the celeriac in salted water for 10 minutes until soft. Drain, put back in the pan and steam-dry for a few minutes. Mash with the butter and some seasoning, then stir in most of the parsley. Keep warm while you cook the fish.

**2** Heat half the oil in a frying pan. Dust the fish in flour, season on both sides, and fry for about 4 minutes on each side. Remove to a plate. Add the remaining oil to the pan, and cook the garlic and chilli for 2 minutes until golden. Add the vinegar, sugar and a little salt, then bubble for 1–2 minutes. Return the fish to the pan to warm through.

**3** Serve the fish on the mash, with the pan sauce poured over. Sprinkle with the remaining parsley and serve with lemon wedges.

---

PER SERVING 259 kcals, protein 25g, carbs 10g, fat 13g, sat fat 5g, fibre 7g, sugar 7g, salt 0.6g

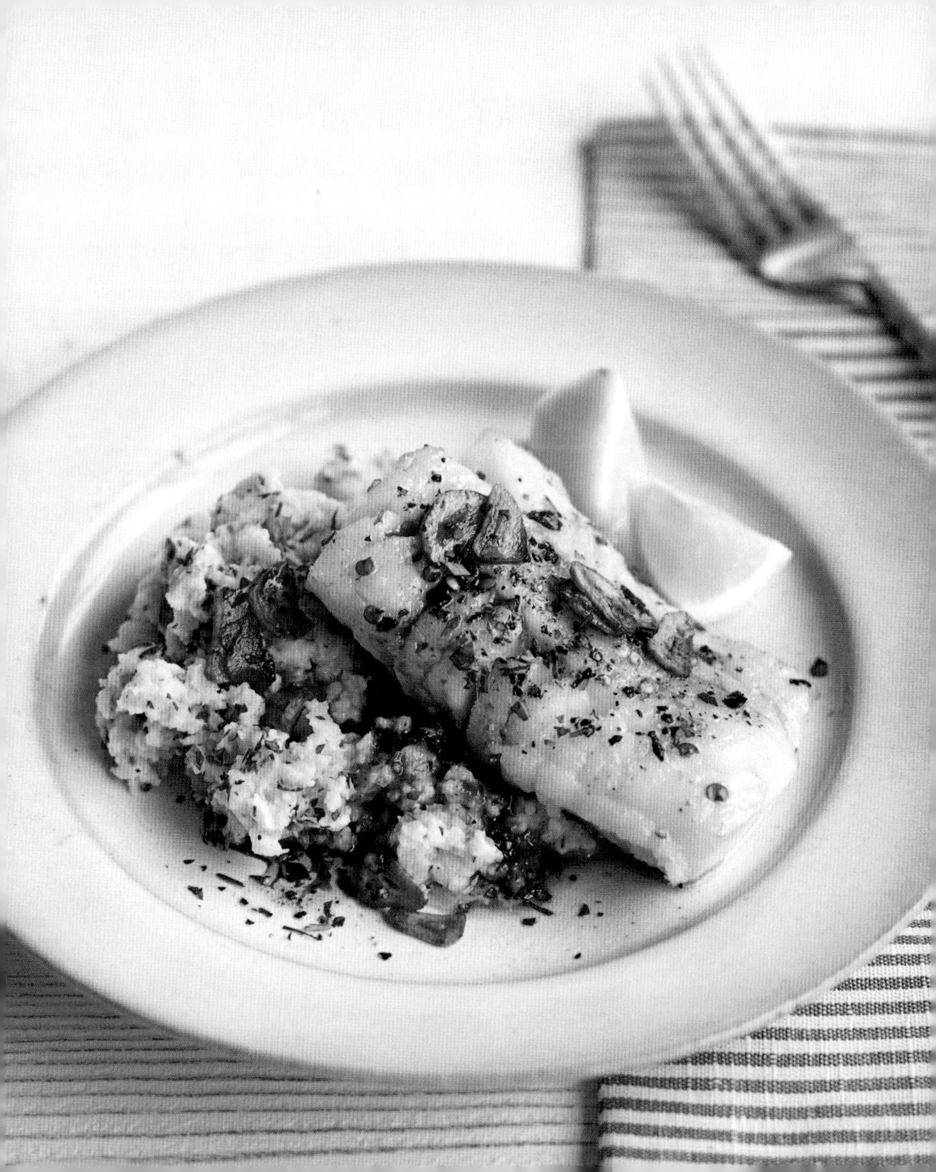

# Spanish seafood pasta

*Love paella? You'll love this easy seafood pasta.*

**TAKES 20 MINUTES • SERVES 4**

350g/12oz short pasta shapes (we used orzo)

1 chicken stock cube

1 tsp turmeric powder or large pinch saffron strands

85g/3oz cooking chorizo, diced

200g pack mixed cooked seafood

2 roasted red peppers, from a jar, sliced

100g/4oz frozen peas

2 tbsp chopped parsley

**1** Cook the pasta in lots of salted, boiling water according to the pack instructions, along with the stock cube and half the turmeric or saffron.

**2** About 7 minutes before the pasta is cooked, tip the chorizo into a frying pan and cook over a medium heat for 5 minutes until slightly crisp. Tip out some of the fat, then add the remaining turmeric or saffron, the seafood, peppers and peas.

**3** Drain the pasta, reserving some of the stock. Tip the pasta back into the pan, add the chorizo-and-seafood mixture and a splash of the reserved stock, and heat through. Stir in most of the parsley.

**4** Serve in warm bowls, with the remaining parsley sprinkled on top.

PER SERVING 429 kcals, protein 24g, carbs 67g, fat 7g, sat fat 3g, fibre 5g, sugar 3g, salt 1.2g

# Bean & pepper chilli

*Use up your storecupboard pulses in this healthy one-pot chilli.*

**TAKES 45 MINUTES • SERVES 4**

1 tbsp olive oil

1 onion, chopped

350g/12oz red peppers, deseeded and sliced

1 tbsp ground cumin

1 tbsp chilli powder

1 tbsp sweet smoked paprika

400g can kidney beans in chilli sauce

400g can mixed beans, drained and rinsed

400g can chopped tomatoes

boiled rice, to serve (optional)

**1** Heat the oil in a large pan. Add the onion and peppers, and cook for 8 minutes until softened. Tip in the spices and cook for 1 minute.

**2** Tip in the beans and tomatoes, bring to the boil and simmer for 15 minutes or until the chilli is thickened. Season and serve with rice, if you like.

---

PER SERVING 183 kcals, protein 11g, carbs 26g, fat 5g, sat fat 1g, fibre 12g, sugar 12g, salt 0.5g

# Spiced carrot, chickpea & almond pilaf

*A healthy budget one-pot. Serve it with warmed naan bread.*

**TAKES 40 MINUTES • SERVES 4**

1 tbsp olive oil

2 onions, finely chopped

3 carrots (about 300g/10oz in total),
   coarsely grated

2 tbsp harissa paste

300g/10oz basmati rice, rinsed

700ml/1¼ pints vegetable stock, made
   with 1 stock cube (or equivalent)

400g can chickpeas, drained and rinsed

25g/1oz toasted flaked almonds

200g pot Greek yogurt

**1** Heat the oil in a lidded casserole dish. Add the onions and cook for 8 minutes, until soft. Tip in the carrots, harissa and rice, and stir for a couple of minutes. Pour over the stock, bring to the boil, then cover with the lid and simmer for 10 minutes.

**2** Fork through the chickpeas and cook gently for 3–5 minutes more, until the grains of rice are tender and all the liquid has been absorbed. Season, turn off the heat, cover and leave to sit for a few minutes.

**3** Sprinkle the almonds over the rice mixture and top with a dollop of yogurt to serve.

PER SERVING 543 kcals, protein 15g, carbs 83g, fat 13g, sat fat 4g, fibre 7g, sugar 14g, salt 1.2g

# Faggots with onion gravy

*Iron-rich faggots are a blast from the thrifty past! Serve with mash and veg, if you like.*

**TAKES 2 HOURS • SERVES 8**

a little oil, for the tin

170g pack sage & onion stuffing mix
(we used Paxo)

500g pack diced pork shoulder

300g/10oz pig livers

½ tsp ground mace

handful chopped parsley, to garnish

mash and veg, to serve (optional)

**FOR THE GRAVY**

2 onions, thinly sliced

1 tbsp sunflower oil

2 tsp sugar

1 tbsp red wine vinegar

3 tbsp plain flour

850ml/1½ pints beef stock

**1** Heat oven to 160C/140C fan/gas 3. Lightly oil a large roasting tin. Tip the stuffing mix into a bowl, add 500ml/ 18fl oz boiling water, stir and set aside.

**2** Pulse the pork in a food processor until finely chopped. Add the livers and pulse again. Add to the stuffing with the mace, 1 teaspoon salt and plenty of black pepper. Stir well. Shape the mixture (it will be very soft) into 24 large faggots and put in the prepared tin.

**3** To make the gravy, fry the onions in the oil until starting to turn golden. Add the sugar and continue cooking, stirring frequently, until caramelised. Tip in the vinegar and allow to sizzle. Mix the flour with 2 tablespoons water. Pour the stock into the onions, then add the flour paste and cook, stirring constantly, until smooth and starting to thicken. When it is thick, pour into the tin with the faggots, cover with foil and bake for 1 hour until cooked through. Serve with a sprinkle of parsley, some mash and veg, if you like.

PER SERVING 208 kcals, protein 26g, carbs 14g, fat 5g, sat fat 1g, fibre 2g, sugar 3g, salt 1.2g

# Chicken katsu

*This dish has become a modern takeaway favourite ever since Japanese fast-food chains started popping up all over the country.*

**TAKES 40 MINUTES • SERVES 4**

4 skinless chicken breasts
1 egg, beaten
8 tbsp finely crushed cornflakes or panko breadcrumbs
2 garlic cloves, crushed
1–2 tbsp korma paste
1 tsp reduced-salt soy sauce
3 tbsp ketchup
2 tbsp honey
2 tbsp cornflour

**1** Heat oven to 200C/180C fan/gas 6. Dip the chicken in the egg, then coat in the cornflakes or breadcrumbs. Space the chicken out on a non-stick baking sheet and cook for 15–20 minutes or until cooked through.

**2** Put the remaining ingredients in a pan. Pour in 500ml/18fl oz water and heat, stirring, until boiling and thickened. Cover and leave to simmer for 5 minutes.

**3** Spoon some sauce on to four plates, slice the chicken breasts and put on top. Great served with some rice and soya beans with finely sliced red chilli.

PER SERVING 318 kcals, protein 34g, carbs 36g, fat 5g, sat fat 1g, fibre 0.3g, sugar 13g, salt 1.5g

# Lemon-scented fish & chips

*Friday fish doesn't have to mean greasy battered cod and oil-laden chips. This lighter version is sure to go down well with the whole family.*

**TAKES 50 MINUTES • SERVES 4**

4 large carrots, cut into thin batons
2 large potatoes, cut into thin batons
few thyme sprigs, leaves picked
1 lemon, zested, then sliced
2 tbsp olive oil
200g/7oz each broccoli florets, frozen
   peas and spinach leaves
2 tbsp crème fraîche
4 white fish fillets

**1** Heat oven to 220C/200C fan/gas 7. Toss the carrots, potatoes, thyme and lemon slices in a large non-stick shallow roasting tin, with the oil and some seasoning. Cook for 25 minutes, shaking the pan once or twice.
**2** Put the broccoli in a pan of boiling water and cook for about 5 minutes or until tender. Stir through the peas and spinach. When all the spinach has wilted and the peas are tender, drain thoroughly. Blitz in a food processor to a smooth purée. Stir through the crème fraîche, a pinch of the lemon zest and some seasoning.
**3** Lay the fish on top of the roasted roots and cook for 15 minutes or so more, until the fish is just cooked through. Make sure the green-veg purée is still hot and serve alongside the fish and roots.

PER SERVING 404 kcals, protein 35g, carbs 33g, fat 15g, sat fat 4g, fibre 9g, sugar 12g, salt 0.6g

# Chicken balti

*If you like your curries spicy, just double the amount of chilli powder and chop up the green chilli with the seeds before adding to the pan.*

**TAKES 55 MINUTES ● SERVES 4**

450g/1lb skinless boneless chicken breasts, cut into bite-sized pieces

1 tbsp lime juice

1 tsp paprika

¼ tsp hot chilli powder

1½ tbsp sunflower or groundnut oil

1 cinnamon stick

3 cardamom pods, split

1 small–medium green chilli

½ tsp cumin seeds

1 onion, coarsely grated

2 garlic cloves, very finely chopped

2.5cm/1in-piece ginger, grated

½ tsp turmeric powder

1 tsp each ground cumin, ground coriander and garam masala

150ml/¼ pint passata

1 red pepper, deseeded, cut into small chunks

1 tomato, chopped

85g/3oz baby leaf spinach

handful fresh coriander, chopped

**1** Put the chicken in a medium bowl. Mix in the lime juice, paprika, chilli powder and a grinding of black pepper.

**2** Heat 1 tablespoon of the oil in a large non-stick pan. Tip in the cinnamon stick, cardamom pods, whole chilli and the cumin seeds, and stir-fry briefly just to colour and release their fragrance. Stir in the onion, garlic and ginger, and fry for 3–4 minutes until the onion starts to brown. Add the remaining oil, then the chicken and stir-fry for 2–3 minutes. Add the ground spices and cook for 2 minutes. Pour in the passata and 150ml/¼ pint water, the chunks of pepper and the tomato. When starting to bubble, lower the heat and simmer for 15–20 minutes.

**3** Add the spinach, turning it over in the pan just to wilt; season. Remove the cinnamon, chilli and cardamom, if you wish. Serve with the coriander garnish.

PER SERVING 217 kcals, protein 30.2g, carbs 10g, fat 7g, sat fat 1g, fibre 3g, sugar 8g, salt 0.5g

# Turkey-coriander burgers with guacamole

*Using turkey mince is a great way to cut the calories, and the vitamin-packed avocado guacamole will give you a great health boost.*

**TAKES 30 MINUTES • SERVES 4**

400g/14oz minced turkey
1 tsp Worcestershire sauce
85g/3oz fresh breadcrumbs
1 tbsp chopped coriander leaves
1 red onion, finely chopped
1 large ripe avocado or 2 small
1 chilli, deseeded and finely chopped
juice 1 lime
4 ciabatta rolls, cut in half
1 tsp sunflower oil
8 hot peppadew peppers, roughly
  chopped

**1** Mix the mince, Worcestershire sauce, breadcrumbs, half each of the coriander and onion, and some seasoning until combined. Form into four burgers, then chill until ready to cook.

**2** To make the guacamole, mash the avocado with the remaining coriander and onion, the chilli and lime juice, and season.

**3** Heat a griddle pan or barbecue until hot. Griddle the rolls, cut-side down, for 1 minute, then keep warm. Brush the burgers with the oil to keep them from sticking. Cook for 7–8 minutes on each side until charred and cooked through. Fill the rolls with the burgers, guacamole and peppadews.

PER SERVING 497 kcals, protein 40g, carbs 51g, fat 15g, sat fat 3g, fibre 6g, sugar 7g, salt 1.3g

# Curry-coconut fish parcels

*Who says you need to spend hours over a hot stove to make a lovely curry? These fish parcels have all the flavour but only take 25 minutes to prepare!*

**TAKES 25 MINUTES • SERVES 2**

2 large tilapia fillets, about 125g/4½oz
    each
2 tsp yellow or red curry paste
2 tsp desiccated coconut
zest and juice 1 lime, plus wedges
    to squeeze over
1 tsp soy sauce
140g/5oz basmati rice
2 tbsp sweet chilli sauce
1 red chilli, deseeded and sliced
cooked thin-stemmed broccoli,
    to serve

**1** Heat oven to 200C/180C fan/gas 6. Tear off four large pieces of foil, double them up, then put a fish fillet in the middle of each. Spread over the curry paste. Divide the coconut, lime zest and juice, and soy between each fillet. Bring up the sides of the foil, then scrunch the edges and sides together to make two sealed parcels.

**2** Put the parcels on a baking sheet and bake for 10–15 minutes. Tip the rice into a pan with plenty of water and boil for 12–15 minutes or until cooked. Drain well. Serve the fish on the rice, drizzle over the chilli sauce and scatter with sliced chilli. Serve with broccoli and lime wedges.

PER SERVING 438 kcals, protein 28g, carbs 63g, fat 6g, sat fat 3g, fibre 2g, sugar 8g, salt 1.3g

# Chicken tikka with spiced rice

*This quick and tasty chicken tikka recipe is a great way to jazz up chicken breasts.*

**TAKES 30 MINUTES, PLUS
MARINATING • SERVES 4**

4 skinless boneless chicken breasts
150g pot low-fat natural yogurt
50g/2oz tikka paste
100g/4oz cucumber, diced
1 tbsp roughly chopped mint leaves
1 red onion, cut into thin wedges
140g/5oz easy-cook long grain rice
1 tbsp medium curry powder
50g/2oz frozen peas
1 small red pepper, deseeded and
   diced

**1** Slash each chicken breast deeply with a knife 3–4 times on one side. Put in a bowl and add 50g/2oz of the yogurt and the tikka paste. Mix well, cover and marinate in the fridge for 30 minutes.
**2** Make the raita by stirring the cucumber and most of the mint into the rest of the yogurt. Season with black pepper, cover and chill.
**3** Heat oven to 240C/220C fan/gas 9. Scatter the onion wedges over a foil-lined roasting tin. Remove the chicken from the marinade, shake off any excess and put on top of the onion wedges. Cook for 20 minutes.
**4** Meanwhile, tip the rice, curry powder, peas and pepper into a pan of boiling water, and simmer for 10 minutes or until the rice is just tender. Drain well and divide the rice among four plates. Add the chicken, roasted onion and remaining mint. Serve with the cucumber raita.

PER SERVING 342 kcals, protein 37g, carbs 38g, fat 5g, sat fat 1g, fibre 4g, sugar 7g, salt 0.7g

# Beef burger & sweet potato-chilli chips

*These spicy sweet potato wedges are a great way to add a fiery kick to your favourite fast-food meal.*

**TAKES 45 MINUTES • SERVES 4**

4 large roundish sweet potatoes, cut into chunky chips
1 tsp olive oil
1 tsp chilli flakes, plus a pinch
400g/14oz pack extra-lean minced beef
1 onion, grated
1 tbsp grated Parmesan
1 tbsp tomato ketchup
4 small wholemeal buns, halved
1 Little Gem lettuce, leaves separated
1 beef tomato, sliced
1 red onion, sliced (optional)
4 pickles or gherkins, halved, to serve

**1** Heat oven to 220C/200C fan/gas 7. Toss the chips with the oil, chilli flakes and some seasoning. Arrange in a single layer on a large baking sheet and cook for about 30 minutes, turning halfway through.

**2** Put the mince, pinch of chilli flakes, onion, Parmesan, tomato ketchup and lots of black pepper in a large bowl, and mix to combine. Shape into four burgers. About 10 minutes before the chips are ready, put the burgers on a baking sheet and bake for 10 minutes until cooked through.

**3** Top one half of each of the buns with the lettuce, tomato and red onion, if using. Add the burgers, then top with the bun lids. Serve with the chips and pickles on the side.

PER SERVING 467 kcals, protein 31g, carbs 57g, fat 13g, sat fat 5g, fibre 7g, sugar 15g, salt 1.3g

# Special fried rice with prawns & chorizo

*Tailor this recipe to whatever suits your children's tastes – you could try adding sweetcorn, broccoli, shredded chicken or bacon.*

**TAKES 30 MINUTES ● SERVES 2**

100g/4oz basmati or long grain rice
85g/3oz frozen peas
1 tbsp sunflower oil
1 egg, beaten
50g/2oz finely diced cooking chorizo, bacon or ham
1 garlic clove, chopped
3 spring onions, sliced on an angle
½ red pepper, deseeded and chopped
good pinch five spice powder
1 tsp soy sauce
100g/4oz beansprouts (optional)
50g/2oz cooked peeled prawns

**1** Boil the rice according to the pack instructions, adding the peas for the final minute. Drain and set aside.

**2** Heat half the oil in a wok. Pour in the egg and stir-fry until scrambled. Tip on to a plate and set aside.

**3** Wipe the wok with kitchen paper, then heat the remaining oil. Toss in the meat, garlic, spring onions and pepper, and stir-fry until the pepper starts to soften. Add the five spice, rice and peas and soy, then stir-fry for 5 minutes more. Finally add the beansprouts, if using, the egg and prawns, and stir-fry to heat through.

PER SERVING 404 kcals, protein 19g, carbs 45g, fat 15g, sat fat 4g, fibre 4g, sugar 5g, salt 1.3g

# No-oven pizza

*Most pizzas use a yeasted bread dough as the base, but this quick version is made with self-raising flour and is cooked in a frying pan to save you time.*

**TAKES 40 MINUTES ● SERVES 4**

225g/8oz self-raising flour
3 tbsp olive oil, plus extra for frying
50g/2oz Chedder, grated

**FOR THE SAUCE**

1 tsp olive oil
1 onion, sliced
3 garlic cloves, crushed
250g pack cherry tomatoes
4 tbsp passata
handful basil leaves, torn, plus extra
   whole leaves to garnish

**1** First make the sauce. Heat the oil in a frying pan, then add the onion and garlic, and cook for 5 minutes. Tip in the tomatoes and passata, and simmer for 5–10 minutes or until the tomatoes are soft. Remove from the heat, stir in the basil, season, then allow to cool.

**2** Put the flour into a bowl. Make a well in the centre, add the olive oil then add 6–7 tablespoons warm water or enough to make a soft dough. Tip the dough on to a lightly floured surface and roll out to fit a 22cm frying pan or make two small ones. Heat a glug of olive oil in the frying pan, then press the dough into the pan and cook over a medium heat for 8–10 minutes or until the base is golden.

**3** Heat grill to hot. Spread the pizza base with the tomato sauce, scatter on the cheese and grill until it has melted and the base is golden at the edges. Serve immediately.

PER SERVING 381 kcals, protein 11g, carbs 47g, fat 18g, sat fat 5g, fibre 3g, sugar 5g, salt 0.33g

# Crispy chicken nuggets

*Kids will love these chunky chicken nuggets – which cleverly use Weetabix to give them a crunchy and nutritious coating.*

**TAKES 30 MINUTES ● SERVES 2**

2 tbsp mayonnaise
2 skinless chicken breast fillets, cut
    into chunks or fingers
25g/1oz fresh breadcrumbs
25g/1oz lightly crushed Weetabix
sauce and chips or salad, to serve

**1** Heat oven to 220C/200C fan/gas 7. Put the mayonnaise in a bowl with the chicken and stir well to coat. Mix the breadcrumbs and Weetabix in another bowl with some seasoning. Tip the crumbs on to a plate and use to coat the chicken.
**2** Spread out the chicken pieces on a baking sheet and bake for 10 minutes until tender but still juicy. Serve with sauce and chips or salad.

PER SERVING 324 kcals, protein 33g, carbs 18g, fat 13g, sat fat 2g, fibre 2g, sugar 1g, salt 0.7g

# Potato & chorizo pizza breads

*A new, healthy way to top a pizza. Sure to become a family favourite.*

**TAKES 20 MINUTES ● MAKES 4**

3 medium–large potatoes, very thinly
  sliced
4 wholemeal tortillas
6 tbsp half-fat crème fraîche
½ onion, thinly sliced
8 thin slices chorizo from a pack, diced
25g/1oz mature Cheddar, grated
3 tomatoes, roughly chopped
2 tsp balsamic dressing
½ tsp coarse black pepper (freshly
  ground)
½ × 50g bag rocket leaves

**1** Heat oven to 200C/180C fan/gas 6.
Bring a pan of water to the boil, then
blanch the potato slices for 2 minutes
until almost cooked. Drain well, then tip
on to kitchen paper to dry.
**2** Put the tortillas on to baking sheets.
Season the crème fraîche, then spread
over the tortillas. Top with the potato
slices, onion and chorizo, then scatter
over the grated cheese.
**3** Bake for 8 minutes until crisp and
golden. Meanwhile, mix the tomatoes
with the dressing and the black pepper,
then toss through the rocket. Pile a
quarter of the salad in the middle of
each tortilla and serve.

PER PIZZA 287 kcals, protein 11g, carbs 37g,
fat 12g, sat fat 5g, fibre 5g, sugar 5g, salt 1.01g

# Pork with sweet & sour onion sauce

*This is a new take on the classic sweet and sour – trust us, it tastes even better than the original!*

**TAKES 30 MINUTES** ● **SERVES 4**

250g/9oz mixed basmati rice and wild rice

600g/1lb 5oz pork fillets, cut into 4cm/1½in-thick slices

2 tbsp coarse black pepper (freshly ground)

2 tbsp olive oil

1 large red onion, halved and sliced

150ml/¼ pint cider vinegar

75ml/2½fl oz maple syrup

small bunch flat-leaf parsley, chopped

**1** Boil the rice in plenty of water, according to the pack instructions, until cooked. Drain, return to the pot and cover to keep warm.

**2** Meanwhile, sprinkle the meat on all sides with the black pepper and some salt. Heat 1 tablespoon of the oil in a large frying pan. Sear the meat on both sides until nicely browned. Remove from the pan.

**3** Add the remaining oil and the onion to the pan. Cook for 5 minutes, then pour in the vinegar and let reduce for 1 minute. Stir in the maple syrup, then return the pork to the pan and heat for 5 minutes until cooked through. Serve the pork and sauce spooned over the rice and scattered with the parsley.

PER SERVING 574 kcals, protein 41g, carbs 61g, fat 16g, sat fat 4g, fibre 3g, sugar 15g, salt 0.2g

# Lemongrass beef stew

*Make sure you keep the fat content low by choosing a cut of beef that is very lean. Trim any fatty bits before cooking.*

**TAKES 2 HOURS** • **SERVES 2**

1 tbsp chopped ginger

2 garlic cloves, chopped

3 lemongrass stalks, outer leaves removed, finely chopped

2 tbsp coriander leaves, plus extra to garnish

2 red chillies, thinly sliced (leave the seeds in if you like it spicy)

2 tbsp vegetable oil

250g/9oz stewing beef, cut into 2.5cm/1in cubes

1 tsp reduced-salt soy sauce

1 tsp five spice powder

1 tsp brown sugar

400ml/14fl oz low-sodium beef stock

100g/4oz wide rice noodles

lime wedges, to squeeze over

**1** Put the ginger, garlic, lemongrass, coriander and 1 of the chillies in a food processor, then pulse until puréed. Heat the oil in a pan over a low heat. Add the purée and cook for 5 minutes. Stir in the beef, soy, five spice, sugar and stock. Put on a lid and bring to the boil, then lower the heat and simmer for 1¼ hours. Remove the lid and cook for a further 15 minutes until the beef is tender.

**2** Just before serving, prepare the noodles according to the pack instructions. Drain well, then divide between two bowls and spoon over the beef stew. Serve sprinkled with the remaining chilli and extra coriander leaves, with the lime wedges for squeezing over.

PER SERVING 497 kcals, protein 35g, carbs 42g, fat 20g, sat fat 5g, fibre 1g, sugar 3g, salt 1g

# Sweetcorn & sweet potato burgers

*In the summer, why not try cooking these burgers on the barbecue? It will give them a lovely smoky flavour and tasty charred edges.*

**TAKES 1½ HOURS • MAKES 10**

6 large sweet potatoes (about
   1.5kg/3lb 5oz in total)
2 tsp oil, plus extra for the tins
2 red onions, finely chopped
2 red chillies, finely chopped
   (deseeded, if you like)
1 tbsp ground cumin
1 tbsp ground coriander
340g can sweetcorn, drained
small bunch coriander, chopped
200g/7oz polenta
buns, salsa, sliced onion and salad
   leaves, to serve

**1** Heat oven to 200C/180C fan/gas 6. Pierce the potato skins and put on a baking sheet. Bake for 45 minutes until really soft. Remove from the oven and leave to cool. Meanwhile, heat the oil in a small pan, add the onions and chillies, and cook for 8–10 minutes until soft. Leave to cool.

**2** Peel the potatoes and add the flesh to a bowl with the chilli onions. Mash together with the spices until smooth. Using your hands, mix in the sweetcorn, coriander, half the polenta and some seasoning. Shape the mixture into 10 burgers. Carefully dip each one into the remaining polenta; dust off any excess. Put the burgers on oiled baking sheets and chill for at least 30 minutes.

**3** Heat oven to 220C/200C fan/gas 7. Cook the burgers on the oiled sheets for 15 minutes, until the edges have crisped up. Serve in buns with a dollop of salsa, some onion and salad leaves.

PER BURGER 252 kcals, protein 5g, carbs 54g, fat 2g, sat fat none, fibre 6g, sugar 12g, salt 0.4g

# Spice-crusted chicken with Asian slaw

*All the flavours of the Orient in a light supper for four.*

**TAKES 25 MINUTES** ● **SERVES 4**
4 skinless boneless chicken breasts
2 tbsp sesame oil
1 tsp each chilli flakes, cumin seeds
    and Sichuan peppercorns
1 tbsp soft brown sugar
1 tbsp soy sauce
juice 1 lemon, plus lemon halves to
    squeeze over
½ small white cabbage, finely shredded
1 red onion, sliced
1 red chilli, deseeded and chopped
small handful coriander sprigs, to
    garnish

**1** Slice most of the way through each chicken breast lengthways and open out like a book. Cover with cling film and gently beat with a rolling pin until flattened. Rub 2 teaspoons of the sesame oil all over the chicken.
**2** Roughly crush the chilli flakes, cumin seeds and peppercorns using a pestle and mortar. Add some salt and sprinkle over both sides of the chicken. Chill until you are ready to cook.
**3** In small bowl, mix the remaining sesame oil, the sugar, soy sauce and lemon juice. Add the cabbage, onion and chilli to a large bowl, pour over half the dressing and mix well. Save the remaining dressing to use as a dipping sauce for the chicken.
**4** Heat grill to high. Put the chicken on a baking sheet lined with foil, grill for 3–4 minutes on each side until cooked through. Serve with the slaw, lemon halves, a scattering of coriander and dipping sauce.

PER SERVING 241 kcals, protein 33g, carbs 12g, fat 7g, sat fat 1g, fibre 3g, sugar 12g, salt 0.9g

# Baked skinny fries

*Your family will never know these fries are baked and not fried – they're supercrispy and incredibly moreish.*

**TAKES 50 MINUTES** ● **SERVES 4**

1 tbsp vegetable oil
2 tsp fine cornmeal or polenta
½ tsp paprika
¼ tsp garlic powder
2 large potatoes, cut into 1cm/½in-
thick chips

**1** Heat oven to 200C/180C fan/gas 6. Pour the oil on to a baking sheet and put it in the oven for 3 minutes. Mix the cornmeal or polenta, paprika and garlic powder together, and season. Toss the chips in the cornmeal mix, then tip on to the sheet. Shake well, then cook for 40 minutes, shaking halfway through, until crisp and golden.

PER SERVING 118 kcals, protein 3g, carbs 20g, fat 3g, sat fat none, fibre 2g, sugar 1g, salt none

# Onion rings

*No American diner-style dinner is complete without crispy onion rings. Serve alongside burger and fries.*

**TAKES 40 MINUTES • SERVES 4**

50g/2oz plain flour
1 large onion, cut into 1cm/½in slices, rings separated
2 egg whites
olive oil, for greasing
2 tsp Cajun seasoning
100g/4oz breadcrumbs

**1** Heat oven to 200C/180C fan/gas 6. Put the flour in a large sealable plastic bag. Season, then tip in the onion and shake well. Whisk the egg whites until foamy, add the onions and stir to coat.
**2** Lightly oil a baking sheet. Add the seasoning and breadcrumbs to the bag; then, working in batches, add the eggy onion rings and coat in the crumbs. Arrange the onion rings, in a single layer, on the baking sheet and cook for 25–30 minutes, turning halfway through, until the onion is tender and the crumbs are golden.

PER SERVING 158 kcals, protein 7g, carbs 32g, fat 1g, sat fat none, fibre 2g, sugar 4g, salt 0.6g

# Super healthy slaw

*This healthy coleslaw is jam-packed with good-for-you veggies. It will keep in the fridge for up to a day.*

**TAKES 15 MINUTES • SERVES 6**

½ Savoy or white cabbage, quartered,
    cored and shredded
1 apple, cored and grated
2 carrots, cut into matchsticks
½ red onion, finely sliced
100g pot fat-free Greek yogurt
juice ½ lemon
2 tsp cider vinegar
2 tsp Dijon mustard

**1** Mix the cabbage, apple, carrots and onion in a large bowl. In a separate bowl, mix the yogurt, lemon juice, vinegar and mustard to make a dressing. Season, then pour over the vegetables. Give everything a good stir to coat in the dressing and eat immediately, or chill until you are ready to serve.

PER SERVING 45 kcals, protein 2g, carbs 8g, fat 1g, sat fat none, fibre 2g, sugar 7g, salt 0.3g

# Roasted stone fruits

*Serve these delicious roasted stone fruits alongside ice cream, yogurt or crème fraîche.*

**TAKES 45 MINUTES • SERVES 8**

3 peaches, halved, stoned and cut into chunky wedges

3 nectarines, halved, stoned and cut into chunky wedges

6 apricots, halved and stoned

400ml/14fl oz Marsala wine

1 tbsp clear honey

50g/2oz butter

**1** Heat oven to 180C/160C fan/gas 4. Toss all the fruits into a snug ovenproof dish or roasting tin. Pour over the Marsala, drizzle over the honey and dot with the butter. Roast for 30 minutes until the fruits are juicy and tender but not mushy.

PER SERVING 174 kcals, protein 2g, carbs 16g, fat 5g, sat fat 3g, fibre none, sugar 14g, salt 0.1g

# Instant frozen-berry yogurt

*Get a healthy, low-fat dessert on the table in 5 minutes!*

**TAKES 5 MINUTES • SERVES 8**
250g/9oz frozen mixed berries
250g/9oz 0%-fat Greek yogurt
1 tbsp clear honey or agave syrup

**1** Blend the berries, yogurt and honey or agave syrup in a food processor for 20 seconds, until it comes together to a smooth ice-cream texture. Scoop into bowls and serve.

PER SERVING 70 kcals, protein 7g, carbs 10g, fat none, sat fat none, fibre 2g, sugar 10g, salt 0.1g

# Cherry-oat squares with choc drizzle

*These fruity oat squares are a great sweet treat for dessert, lunchboxes or cake sales.*

**TAKES 45 MINUTES**

● **CUTS INTO 16 SQUARES**

140g/5oz butter, melted, plus extra butter for the tin

100g/4oz self-raising flour

140g/5oz caster sugar

175g/6oz porridge oats

1 medium egg, beaten

85g/3oz glacé cherries, halved

50g/2oz dark chocolate

**1** Heat oven to 180C/160C fan/gas 4. Butter and line the base and sides of a 22cm-square cake tin: cut two strips of baking parchment the width of the tin and longer than the base and sides, and fit into the tin each way and up the sides. This will make lifting out the squares easier.

**2** Mix together the flour, sugar and oats in a bowl. Add the egg, melted butter and cherries, and mix well. Tip into the tin and spread evenly with a fork.

**3** Bake for 20–25 minutes until golden brown. Cool in the tin for 10 minutes, then carefully lift out using the paper and put on a board. Mark, but don't cut, four lines each way to make 16 squares. Melt the chocolate in the microwave on Medium for 1 minute, then drizzle over the squares. When the chocolate has set, cut the squares down the marked lines.

PER SQUARE 196 kcals, protein 3g, carbs 24g, fat 9g, sat fat 5g, fibre 2g, sugar 14g, salt 0.2g

# Lightest meringues

*Candy-coloured giant meringues are all the rage in top patisseries, and they contain no fat, so you can enjoy them guilt free!*

**TAKES 1 HOUR 25 MINUTES**
● **MAKES 18**
4 egg whites
225g/8oz caster sugar
1 tsp vanilla extract
¼ tsp food colouring (optional)

**1** Heat oven to 140C/120C fan/gas 1. Line two baking sheets with baking parchment. Whisk the egg whites until very stiff. Once you have reached this point, pour in roughly half the sugar and the vanilla extract, and whisk again until the mixture becomes very thick, firm and shiny. Add the remaining sugar and whisk again until thick, firm and shiny. Add your food colouring, if using, and ripple through with a spoon.

**2** Spoon mounds of the meringue on to your lined sheets. Bake in the oven for 1 hour, turning the heat down to 120C/100C fan/gas ½ after 30 minutes.

**3** Remove from the oven – they should easily peel away from the parchment – and cool on a wire rack. Can be made up to a week ahead and kept in an airtight container, or frozen for up to 3 months, between layers of parchment in an airtight container.

PER MERINGUE 53 kcals, protein 1g, carbs 13g, fat none, sat fat none, fibre none, sugar 13g, salt 0.04g

# Chocolate-cardamom pots

*Chocolate and cardamom is an interesting flavour combination, and these little pots are perfect for a special dessert.*

**TAKES 20 MINUTES • MAKES 4**
25g/1oz white chocolate
50g/2oz dark chocolate, chopped
2 egg whites
1 tbsp caster sugar
generous pinch ground cardamom

**1** Make chocolate curls with the white chocolate by running a swivel peeler over the surface. When you have enough to sprinkle over four chocolate pots, set these aside, then chop the remainder.

**2** Melt the dark chocolate in a heatproof bowl over a pan of simmering water or in the microwave on Medium for 1½–2 minutes. Leave to cool slightly. Whisk the egg whites until stiff, then whisk in the sugar and cardamom. Fold in the melted chocolate, then gently fold in the chopped white chocolate.

**3** Divide among four small dishes or cups, about 100ml in size. Sprinkle over the white-chocolate curls and chill until ready to serve, at least 1 hour.

PER POT 119 kcals, protein 3g, carbs 16g, fat 5g, sat fat 3g, fibre none, sugar 15g, salt 0.11g

# Rock cakes

*A tea-time classic, perfect for making with kids.*

**TAKES 45 MINUTES • MAKES 10**

200g/7oz self-raising flour
1 tsp baking powder
1½ tsp ground mixed spice
100g/4oz cold butter
85g/3oz light muscovado sugar
100g/4oz mixed dried fruit
1 egg, beaten
2 tbsp milk
demerara sugar or roughly crushed
    sugar cubes, for sprinkling

**1** Heat oven to 180C/160C fan/gas 4. Line a baking sheet with baking parchment. Tip the flour, baking powder and 1 teaspoon of the mixed spice into a bowl. Add the butter, cut into small pieces. Rub the butter into the flour until the mixture forms fine crumbs (or do this in the food processor).

**2** Stir in the muscovado sugar and fruit; then add the egg and milk. Mix to a fairly firm dough. Spoon 10 rough blobs of the mixture on to the baking sheet, leaving room between each blob for a little spreading. Mix together the sugar and remaining mixed spice, and sprinkle over the cakes. Bake for 20–25 minutes until golden brown.

PER CAKE 211 kcals, protein 3g, carbs 29g, fat 9g, sat fat 5g, fibre 1g, sugar 15g, salt 0.5g

# Smoothie jellies

*A clever way to transform a healthy smoothie into a tasty dessert.*

**TAKES 10 MINUTES, PLUS SETTING**
- **MAKES 12**

6 sheets leaf gelatine
1 litre bottle orange, mango and
    passion fruit smoothie (we used
    Innocent)
ice cream, to serve (optional)

**1** Put the leaf gelatine into a bowl and cover with cold water. Leave for a few minutes until soft and floppy.

**2** Meanwhile, gently heat the smoothie in a pan without boiling. Take off the heat. Lift the gelatine out of the water, squeeze out the excess water, then add it to the smoothie pan. Stir well until smooth, then pour into 12 moulds, pots or glasses. Chill for at least 1 hour to set.

**3** Serve each smoothie jelly topped with ice cream, if you like.

PER SERVING (1 jelly and 1 tbsp ice cream)
92 kcals, protein 4g, carbs 15g, fat 2g, sat fat 1g,
fibre 2g, sugar 13g, salt 0.05g

# Pretzel-popcorn squares

*The perfect sweet snack for family film night.*

**TAKES 15 MINUTES, PLUS CHILLING**
**• MAKES 12**

300g/10oz marshmallows
140g/5oz plain popcorn
200g/7oz pretzels, roughly chopped

**1** Put the marshmallows in a pan and melt, stirring continuously. Stir in the popcorn and pretzels. Pour on to a baking sheet lined with baking parchment, roughly 23cm × 33cm, and chill until set. Cut into squares with a sharp knife to serve.

---

PER SQUARE 214 kcals, protein 3g, carbs 37g, fat 6g, sat fat 1g, fibre none, sugar 15g, salt 0.7g

# Little toffee-apple cake

*We all need a sweet treat, even when trying to eat well. This lovely toffee-apple cake is sin free.*

**TAKES 1 HOUR 10 MINUTES • CUTS INTO 8 SLICES**

3 tbsp sunflower oil, plus more for the tin

1 large apple, peeled and grated

1 egg

1 tsp vanilla extract

100g/4oz self-raising flour

50g/2oz golden caster sugar

3 soft toffees

**1** Heat oven to 190C/170C fan/ gas 5. Brush a small 500g loaf tin with a little oil.

**2** Put the grated apple in a large bowl and add the egg, oil and vanilla. Mix well, then add the flour and sugar, and stir to combine.

**3** Scrape the mixture into the prepared tin then push the toffees into the mix in a row. Cook for 30–40 minutes, then leave to cool in the tin before removing to a wire rack and slicing.

PER SLICE 145 kcals, protein 2g, carbs 21g, fat 6g, sat fat 1g, fibre 1g, sugar 10g, salt 0.18g

# Skinny chocolate & cranberry muffins

*Kids and adults alike will love these chocolatey treats. Pop any extras into lunchboxes.*

**TAKES 35 MINUTES • MAKES 12**

250g/9oz self-raising flour
1 tbsp cocoa powder
1 tsp baking powder
1 tsp ground cinnamon
75g/2½oz light muscovado sugar
50g/2oz dried cranberries
25g/1oz dark chocolate, chopped
125g tub low-fat yogurt
125ml/4fl oz skimmed milk
3 tbsp sunflower oil
1 egg, lightly beaten

**1** Heat oven to 180C/160C fan/gas 4. Line a 12-hole muffin tin with paper cases. Sift the flour, cocoa, baking powder and cinnamon into a bowl. Stir in the sugar and cranberries. Microwave the chocolate on Medium for 1–1½ minutes, stir, then set aside.
**2** Mix the yogurt and milk with the oil and egg. Make a well in the centre of the dry mix and gently stir in the liquid. Drizzle half the chocolate over the mix, gently fold in until swirled, then repeat with the remaining chocolate. Take care not to over-mix. Spoon the mix into the muffin cases and bake for 15–20 minutes until risen and firm to the touch.

PER MUFFIN 162 kcals, protein 4g, carbs 27g, fat 5g, sat fat 1g, fibre 1g, sugar 12g, salt 0.4g

# Healthy banana bread

*Everyone loves banana bread, whether it's for pud with ice cream and chocolate sauce or for breakfast with a little butter.*

**TAKES 1 HOUR 35 MINUTES • CUTS INTO 10 SLICES**

low-fat spread, for the tin, plus extra to serve

140g/5oz wholemeal flour

100g/4oz self-raising flour

1 tsp bicarbonate of soda

1 tsp baking powder

300g/10oz mashed bananas (from over-ripe black bananas)

4 tbsp agave syrup

3 eggs, beaten with a fork

150g pot low-fat natural yogurt

25g/1oz chopped pecan nuts or walnuts (optional)

**1** Heat oven to 160C/140C fan/gas 3. Grease and line a 900g loaf tin with baking parchment (allow it to come 2cm/¾in above the top of the tin). Mix the flours, bicarbonate of soda, baking powder and a pinch of salt in a large bowl.

**2** Mix together the bananas, syrup, eggs and yogurt. Quickly stir this into the dry ingredients, then gently scrape into the tin and scatter with nuts, if using. Bake for 1 hour 10 minutes–1¼ hours or until a skewer inserted into the centre comes out clean.

**3** Cool in the tin on a wire rack. Eat warm or at room temperature, with low-fat spread.

PER SLICE 132 kcals, protein 5g, carbs 22g, fat 2g, sat fat 1g, fibre 3g, sugar 7g, salt 0.6g

# Lighter chocolate mousses

*If your children prefer sweeter chocolate, use milk chocolate or a dark one with a lower percentage of cocoa solids.*

**TAKES 20 MINUTES ● MAKES 4**

85g/3oz dark chocolate, 70% cocoa solids, very finely chopped
1 tbsp cocoa powder, plus extra for dusting
½ tsp coffee granules
½ tsp vanilla extract
2 egg whites
1 tbsp golden caster sugar
50g/2oz full-fat Greek yogurt
handful raspberries, to decorate

**1** Put the chocolate into a large bowl that will fit over a pan of simmering water. Mix the cocoa, coffee and vanilla with 2 tablespoons cold water, and pour over the chocolate. Put the bowl over the gently simmering water, give it all a stir, then remove the pan from the heat. Stir the chocolate occasionally until melted.

**2** Stir in 2 tablespoons boiling water to the thick melted chocolate to thin down. Leave to cool slightly.

**3** Whisk the egg whites to fairly soft peaks, then whisk in the sugar until thick and glossy. Beat the yogurt into the cooled chocolate. Fold about one-third of the egg whites into the chocolate mix using a large metal spoon, then very gently fold in the rest of the whites until they are evenly mixed in. Spoon into four small cups or ramekins and chill for a couple of hours, or overnight, until set.

**4** Top with raspberries, then dust with cocoa powder and serve.

PER MOUSSE 167 kcals, protein 4g, carbs 15g, fat 10g, sat fat 5g, fibre 2g, sugar 11g, salt 0.12g

# Index

agave, pistachio & grapefruit
    salad 14–15
almond
    butter 46–7
    carrot & chickpea pilaf 148–9
apple
    & linseed porridge 12–13
    toffee, little cakes 204–5
apricot, honey & pistachio bars
    34–5
arrabiata, chicken 128–9
asparagus soldiers 22–3
aubergine, pepper & bulghar
    charred salad 110–11
avocado
    chicken & carrot rolls 104–5
    & crab wrap 106–7
    cream 120–1
    & turkey toasts 62–3

bacon
    egg & bean bread bake 40–1
    lettuce, peas & cod 118–19
bagels, salmon & chive 102–3
balti, chicken 156–7
banana
    healthy bread 208–9
    & peanut butter toastie 36–7
barley, chicken & mushroom
    risotto 134–5
bean(s)
    bacon & egg bread bake 40–1
    better-than-baked 42–3
    & chicken spicy wrap 88–9
    & courgette minty dip 50–1

& pepper chilli 146–7
    & rice Mexican salad 94–5
    warm Mexican dip 48–9
beef
    burger, & chips 164–5
    lemongrass stew 176–7
    more veg bolognese 126–7
beetroot
    carrot & chickpea pittas 98–9
    potato & pollack traybake 122–3
berries, frozen yogurt 190–1
bolognese, more veg 126–7
bread
    bean, bacon & egg bake 40–1
    flowerpot 66–7
    healthy banana 208–9
bulghar, aubergine & pepper
    charred salad 110–11
burgers
    beef, & chips 164–5
    sweetcorn & sweet potato
        178–9
    turkey coriander 158–9
butter, almond 46–7

cakes
    little toffee apple 204–5
    rock 198–9
    spiced fruit loaf 32–3
    see also muffins
carrot
    avocado & chicken roll 104–5
    chickpea & beetroot pitta 98–9
    spiced, pilaf 148–9
celeriac parsley mash 142–3

cheese, Scandi, & crackers 58–9
cherry oat squares 192–3
chicken
    arrabiata 128–9
    balti 156–7
    & bean spicy wrap 88–9
    carrot & avocado rolls 104–5
    chickpea salad 86–7
    crispy nuggets 170–1
    katsu 152–3
    mushroom & barley risotto
        134–5
    pesto pasta salad 96–7
    & rice Mexican soup 82–3
    spice-crusted, & slaw 180–1
    sweetcorn & noodle soup 84–5
    tikka, & rice 162–3
chickpea
    almond & carrot spiced pilaf
        148–9
    beetroot & carrot pittas 98–9
    chicken salad 86–7
    spicy 60–1
chilli, bean & pepper 146–7
chips
    & lemon-scented fish 154–5
    sweet potato chilli 164–5
chocolate
    cardamom pots 196–7
    & cranberry muffins 206–7
    lighter mousse 210–11
chorizo
    & potato pizza breads 172–3
    prawns & fried rice 166–7
coconut curry fish parcels 160–1

cod
  bacon, lettuce & peas 118–19
  sticky, & celeriac mash 142–3
compote, summer fruit 16–17
cookies, oat energies 64–5
courgette
  fritters 72–3
  & minty bean dip 50–1
  & tomato soup 80–1
crab & avocado wrap 106–7
crackers & Scandi cheese 58–9
cranberry & choc muffins 206–7
curry 86–7, 156–7, 160–3

dips
  courgette & minty bean 50–1
  pea, mint & chilli 52–3
  warm Mexican bean 48–9
dressings
  balsamic 132–3
  curry yogurt 86–7
  yogurt 98–9

egg
  bean & bacon bread bake 40–1
  dippy, & Marmite soldiers 24–5
  one-pan summer 18–19
  soft-boiled, & asparagus
    soldiers 22–3
  spiced scrambled 20–1
  veggie breakfast bakes 38–9

faggots with onion gravy 150–1
fajitas, prawn & avocado 120–1
falafel, spinach & feta 74–5
feta & spinach falafel 74–5
fish & chips, lemon 154–5
fries, baked skinny 182–3
fruit

fruitburst muffins 30–1
  roasted stone 188–9
  spiced loaf 32–3
  summer, compote 16–17

granola, good-for-you 10–11
grapefruit, agave & pistachio
    salad 14–15
gravy, onion 150–1
guacamole 158–9

haddock, smoked, kedgeree 44–5

jellies, smoothie 200–1

kale, ricotta, tomato & pesto
    pasta 138
kedgeree, classic 44–5

lentil lasagne 136–7
lettuce, pea, bacon & cod 118–19

meatballs, baked turkey 116–17
meringues, lightest 194–5
minestrone, spring 78–9
mousse, light chocolate 210–11
muffins
  choc & cranberry 206–7
  fruitburst 30–1
mushroom
  barley & chicken risotto 134–5
  & tomato pancakes 26–7
  veggie breakfast bakes 38–9

noodle
  chicken & sweetcorn soup 84–5
  prawn, crunchy salad 112–13

oat(s)

cherry squares 192–3
  oaty energy cookies 64–5
  raspberry traybake 56–7
onion
  gravy 150–1
  rings 184–5
  sweet & sour sauce 174–5

pancakes
  plate-sized 28–9
  tomato & mushroom 26–7
Parmesan potato skins 68–9
pasta
  cherry tomato, kale & ricotta
    pesto 138
  chicken arrabiata 128–9
  lentil lasagne 136–7
  more veg bolognese 126–7
  salad, chicken pesto 96–7
  salad, tuna, capers & balsamic
    dressing 132–3
  Spanish seafood 144–5
pea
  bacon, lettuce & cod 118–19
  mint & chilli dip 52–3
peanut butter & banana toastie
    36–7
pepper
  & bean chilli 146–7
  bulghar & aubergine salad 110–11
pesto
  cherry tomato, kale & ricotta
    pasta 138
  chicken pasta salad 96–7
pilaf, spiced carrot 148–9
pistachio, apricot & honey bars
    34–5
pittas, beetroot, carrot &
    chickpea 98–9

Index   213

pizza, no-oven 168–9
pizza bread, potato & chorizo 172–3
pollack, beetroot & potato traybake 122–3
popcorn pretzel squares 202–3
pork & onion sauce 174–5
porridge, apple & linseed 12–13
potato
    baked skinny fries 182–3
    & chorizo pizza breads 172–3
    crispy, & meatballs 116–17
    Parmesan skins 68–9
    pollack & beetroot bake 122–3
    stuffed jackets 90–1
    turkey chilli jackets 130–1
    wedges 42–3
prawn
    & avocado fajitas 120–1
    chorizo & fried rice 166–7
    cocktail, open sandwich 92–3
    noodle, crunchy salad 112–13
    skewers, & rice salad 124–5
pretzel popcorn squares 202–3

quinoa tuna spicy salad 108–9

raspberry oat traybake 56–7
rice 44–5, 134–5, 148–9, 174–5
    & bean Mexican salad 94–5
    & chicken soup 82–3
    chicken tikka with 162–3
    salad, & prawns 124–5
    special fried 166–7
ricotta, cherry tomato & kale pesto pasta 138
risotto, barley, chicken & mushroom 134–5
rock cakes 198–9

salad
    charred pepper, bulghar & aubergine 110–11
    chicken chickpea 86–7
    crunchy prawn noodle 112–13
    grapefruit, agave & pistachio 14–15
    Mexican rice & bean 94–5
    pasta, tuna & caper 132–3
    pesto chicken pasta 96–7
    rainbow tomato 100–1
    rice, & prawn skewers 124–5
    spicy tuna quinoa 108–9
salmon
    & chive bagel topper 102–3
    grilled, tacos 114–15
sandwich, prawn cocktail 92–3
seafood Spanish pasta 144–5
seed mix, Chinese-spiced 54–5
slaw
    Asian 180–1
    super healthy 186–7
smoothie jellies 200–1
soup
    chicken & noodle 84–5
    courgette & tomato 80–1
    Mexican chicken & rice 82–3
    spring minestrone 78–9
    Thai squash 76–7
spinach & feta falafel 74–5
squash, Thai soup 76–7
stew, lemongrass beef 176–7
sweet potato
    chilli chips 164–5
    & sweetcorn burgers 178–9
sweetcorn
    noodle & chicken soup 84–5
    & sweet potato burgers 178–9
    tuna cakes 140–1

tacos, grilled salmon 114–15
tilapia parcels, curry coconut 160–1
toastie, peanut butter & banana 36–7
toasts, turkey & avocado 62–3
toffee apple little cakes 204–5
tomato
    cherry, kale & ricotta pesto pasta 138
    & courgette soup 80–1
    & mushroom pancakes 26–7
    rainbow salad 100–1
tortillas
    Cajun tortilla chips 70–1
    chicken, carrot & avocado 104–5
    crab & avocado 106–7
    grilled salmon tacos 114–15
    potato & chorizo pizza 172–3
    prawn & avocado fajitas 120–1
    spicy chicken & bean 88–9
tuna
    capers & balsamic dressing with pasta salad 132–3
    quinoa spicy salad 108–9
    sweetcorn cakes 140–1
turkey
    & avocado toasts 62–3
    baked meatballs, broccoli & crispy potatoes 116–17
    chilli jacket potatoes 130–1
    coriander burgers 158–9

yogurt
    chipotle lime 114–15
    curry dressing 86–7
    dressing 98–9
    instant frozen berry 190–1

## Also available from BBC Books and *Good Food*

**Baking**
Cakes & Bakes
Chocolate Treats
Cupcakes & Small Bakes
Easy Baking Recipes
Fruity Puds
Teatime Treats
Tempting Desserts
**Easy**
30-minute Suppers
Budget Dishes
Cheap Eats
Easy Student Dinners
Easy Weeknight Suppers
More One-pot Dishes
One-pot Dishes
Simple Suppers
Speedy Suppers
Slow Cooker Favourites
**Everyday**
Best-ever Chicken Recipes
Best-ever Curries
Fish & Seafood Dishes
Gluten-free Recipes
Hot & Spicy Dishes
Italian Feasts
Low-carb Cooking
Meals for Two
Mediterranean Dishes
Pasta & Noodle Dishes
Picnics & Packed Lunches
Recipes for Kids
Stir-fries & Quick Fixes
Storecupboard Suppers
**Healthy**
Healthy Eats
Low-fat Feasts
More Low-fat Feasts
Seasonal Salads
Superhealthy Suppers
Veggie Dishes
**Weekend**
Barbecues and Grills
Christmas Dishes
Delicious Gifts
Dinner-party Dishes
Make Ahead Meals
Slow-cooking Recipes
Soups & Sides